GET INTO A TOP BUSINESS SCHOOL

50+
SUCCESSFUL
WHARTON
BUSINESS SCHOOL
ESSAYS

◆

Write a successful application essay
that gets you accepted to the world's top business schools

◆

Library of Congress Control Number:

ISBN 13:   978-0615606583
ISBN 10:   061560658X

ACKNOWLEDGEMENT

The business school application process is an increasingly competitive and daunting experience. With the advent of internet forums and advisors, the noise around creating a good business school application has increased, as has the misinformation on the traits or buzzwords a top business school is looking for in an application. *50+ Successful Wharton Business School Essays* was designed to provide an unbiased source for examples of the multitude of successful applicants and application styles.

While commentary on essay questions is included in *50+ Successful Wharton Business School Essays,* this book shies away from attempting to explain why a person or essay was successful. It is by definition an impossible task given these essays are just one part of overall impressive applications of accomplished professionals, artists, and public servants. While the essays were selected for their thoughtfulness and variety, it is a common refrain among admissions committees that some students were admitted *in spite* of their essays, not because of them.

This book was created by Wharton Business School students. These are their ideas solely and not those of the school. Like this book, the school feels that there is not one single way to write a great essay. Note that the views, values and recent developments of the school are easily found on the Wharton school website and by speaking with current students and administrators. This approach is highly recommended.

A huge thanks goes out to the many students, faculty and friends who have supported this book coming to fruition and graciously contributed their stories and feedback. Without the strong Wharton community, this would never have been possible.

Last, Wharton believes strongly in community engagement and works closely with a number of outstanding nonprofit organizations in the Philadelphia area. These critical nonprofits support such efforts as literacy and home refurbishment in underserved areas. A portion of the proceeds from this book will go to these essential causes.

Bredesen Lewis

TABLE OF CONTENTS

INTRODUCTION

There is little doubt that applying to business school is a long, arduous and at times frustrating process. To a large extent, your application has been constructed over many years. It is difficult to control where you were born and have lived, what undergraduate school you attended, the GPA you got, and the job you have done for half of a decade.

What is different and exceptional about business school, unlike other graduate level schools, is that the lessons you have learned and your personal "story" and journey matter tremendously. What differentiates you from all of the other applicants who are similar on paper is your ability to lucidly and convincingly paint this portrait. Through your business school application essays, you must be able to convey the core of who you are, the specific experiences that you have lived until today, and the insights you have gleaned over the past five or ten years.

Top business schools are looking for many things. Increasingly, this is not what the stereotype of a business person used to be (while top schools will remain successful with Wall Street, nobody wants a Gordon Gekko or another Enron). An increased focus on social responsibility and business' interaction with the broader society means that future business leaders must be thoughtful and self-aware. Being clever and hard working is no longer enough in today's interconnected world.

Top business schools such as Wharton are looking for a diverse student body that represents the society and world we live in. This means a higher concentration of women and minorities, a student body with a global footprint, and leaders in fields from industry, to start-ups, to nonprofit organizations and public service.

As anyone who is deeply involved in the business school application process knows, there is a large business that has sprung up around business school applications and getting you into a top school. Some applicants, having worked for a few years, are flush with cash, while others are willing to pay whatever it takes for the promise of large salaries. While these services can provide useful advice to some, the emergence of expensive business school advisors is a mixed bag. As in music or sports, having a good coach is not something to be scoffed at. Nonetheless, that some applicants pay thousands of dollars while others may not be able to is not only an uneven playing field but can distort the essence of an application in search of a perceived ideal that no longer exists amongst the top schools.

This book is designed to even the playing field and allow students to tell an honest story. While there is no panacea or silver bullet in business school applications, coming across as authentic, thoughtful and polished is a strong combination. This book is designed to provide examples of successful essays that demonstrate the diversity of experiences people have had and portray the commonalities in self-reflection and personal growth that admissions committees are looking for. Every person's story is different and this book should only be another tool in your application process. It will always be the case that peer editors who know you well, the process of brainstorming, and the time and quiet to reflect on a meaningful and authentic story of who you are is the truest recipe for success.

PART I
WHARTON ESSAYS

PROFESSIONAL OBJECTIVES

What are your professional objectives? (300 words)

INTRODUCTION

One thing that is constant about business school is change. Largely for the better, there is a tremendous amount of opportunity for students attending a top business school program. That's much of the value in going!

More than anything, the career goal essay is simply to be sure that you have thought about what you might like to do, how your experiences could be leveraged to achieve the target, and what steps you might take in the near future to further that goal. As such, it is a great time for reflection. Be thoughtful and honest but do not fear if you are torn between working for a cause you believe in and joining McBain. It is a common dilemma facing business school students. However, a word to the wise...

Wharton is among the best business schools in the world and any field you might like to enter is a very serious option. It may sound great but that is also the problem. If you do not come to the program with a vague idea of things you might be interested in, you will be pulled in a hundred directions (that will happen anyway) and miss out on valuable opportunities to hone the skills that matter to you.

As you will see in these essays, there are many ways to craft your story and motivation. You will see some recurring themes, including working internationally, social impact, and expanding beyond professional services. These are common interests amongst students at Wharton but in no way mandatory. In fact, a well written essay on why you want to be a hedge fund manager can be just as compelling as eradicating hunger in India.

The point is to be authentic, connect the dots, and take the time to research and revise your work. You will see that some of the essays that pop the most mention three things: relevant facts about a person's experience, specific ideas on what role or organization they might like to join in the future, and possibly concrete examples of why Wharton could facilitate that success. Use these guidelines to go forth and write a great essay!

The Career Changer

I intend to pursue a career as an investment professional specializing in private equity investments. I believe the mixture of experience in advising financial sponsors in connection with acquisitions, dispositions and recapitalizations that I already have acquired, combined with the quantitative and management skills I hope to hone at The Wharton School of the University of Pennsylvania, will leave me uniquely positioned to make wise investment decisions. Beyond passive investment decision-making, however, it is important to me to be a part of a team that takes an active role in improving the performance of portfolio companies by collaborating with their management teams and providing strategic assistance throughout the course of the relationship. During my career as a corporate attorney, I have been exposed to a myriad of successful and unsuccessful private equity investments, and, everything else being equal, it seems that the difference often comes down to the level of support provided by the private equity teams to their portfolio companies. Results aside, I'm confident that I will experience greater professional satisfaction if my firm values working with its portfolio companies rather than simply viewing them as a means to an end. For that reason, I plan to work for an equity fund manager that devotes its capital to middle market investments that offer the most room for creative approaches and non-traditional value creation. As a significant portion of my last four years has been dedicated to counseling privately held companies on a broad range of general corporate, securities laws and corporate governance matters, I believe I will be well-suited to assisting portfolio companies realize their full potential after completing my studies at the Wharton School. While I will appreciate the legal knowledge, drafting expertise and interpersonal skills I have developed while acting as an advisor, my passion is to be a part of a team that makes and executes its own decisions and has its results determined by the success or failure of such decisions.

▶ EDITOR'S NOTE

This applicant demonstrates a very clear vision of how his career in law will directly relate to his well defined ambitions post-business school.

From Military to Clean Tech

On the flight back from one of my Middle-East deployments, I read Thomas Friedman's *Hot, Flat and Crowded*. His chapter, "Out-Greening Al Qaeda" regarding alternative energy and its potential effect on the US military, struck me deeply. Having witnessed firsthand the cost of the military's fossil-fuel dependence, in both money and lives, I am convinced our armed services owe it to both the country and the world to lead the conversion to alternative energy.

My post-MBA career vision is to promote the "greening of the military", as an aerospace and defense consultant at firms such as Booz Allen or McKinsey. There I will use my military experience and MBA analytical skills to transform firms supporting our armed forces through energy-efficient methodologies. In the long term, I will build on my consulting career, combined with my development experience as a civil affairs officer in Afghanistan and my French fluency developed in the Lauder program, to lead a venture capital firm promoting sustainable growth projects in Francophone Africa. My vision is to encourage the stable development of impoverished regions such as Algeria, Côte d'Ivoire, or Senegal, to prevent them from becoming the next American battleground.

In 2002, while attending military training, the base newspaper covered Wharton Leadership Venture students learning military leadership skills at our training center, sparking my early interest in its MBA program. Having since met countless Wharton veterans, I associate the school's name with a vigorous exchange of ideas between the military and business worlds. I joined the military to shape foreign policy as a US Marine. Now I hope to leverage my military leadership and international exposure, combined with the Wharton MBA and Lauder MA, to shape the world through business.

From McBain to Bollywood and Back

My professional objective is to be a recognized authority on international Media & Entertainment, influencing where and how the world's M&E companies invest in international markets.

My objective is personal. After a childhood immersed in Bollywood films and a year working in media in Mumbai, I'm excited about growth from new markets – like fast-growing, film-crazy India. I also believe in the media's social power, particularly in developing countries: I've developed a comedy segment to promote India-Pakistan peace for MTV Style Guru, and am currently producing a documentary on religious coexistence with Yusuf Islam (Cat Stevens).

My role models are many: Sony Pictures CEO Michael Lynton for his commitment to growth from local content in global markets (after the Chinese *Crouching Tiger Hidden Dragon*, he delivered the first Hollywood/Bollywood co-production in 2007); John Miller of J.P. Morgan, Hollywood's top banker, for the revolutionary financial modeling and innovative financing methods he's used to back countless Oscar winners; and Jeff Skoll, Participant Media chairman, for producing profitable films with social conscience, such as Al Gore's *An Inconvenient Truth, The Kite Runner, and Darfur Now.*

Observing these visionaries, I've learned important lessons in M&E about growth in emerging markets, financial viability, and social responsibility. After gaining McBain consulting knowledge I have had varied media experiences, which include working as production manager for MTV Pakistan. Post-MBA, I will build a foundation in the strategic and financial sides of global M&E at a leader like Disney (business development), the industry-dominating Media-Technology group at J.P. Morgan, or a media-focused investment bank like Allen and Co. In the intermediate-term, I will gain international exposure while managing an international division of a Big Six M&E company. Ultimately, as an authority on international growth in M&E, I hope to lead a major studio like Sony or a progressive independent studio like Participant, or head corporate strategy/development at a major M&E company.

▶ ## EDITOR'S NOTE

This applicant makes great use of showing how a typical consulting role led to a much richer and more colorful interest in media and how these two might join again after Wharton.

Dedication to Technology and Development

My previous experiences have taught me that pursuing my keen interests brings me fulfillment and exhorts me to excel in my endeavors. Today, my objective is to act upon my strongest passions in life: family business, entrepreneurship and social work.

In the next five to ten years, I see myself growing the family business to become the Middle East's leading cosmetics manufacturer. Joining my parents' company has been a desire of mine ever since I started advising the business on key strategic issues. In the last six months, using my consulting experience, I have helped the company navigate through very challenging times. In particular, I produced the business plan that secured a sorely needed $5 million dollar loan. This experience has shown me that the company lacks the strategic focus and essential functions such as marketing or human resources to attain its true potential. However, it also clarified for me how entrepreneurial the family business is, and how much I want to be part of it.

In a later stage, I plan to contribute to the development of my country and region. Building upon the entrepreneurial experience and financial assets I will accumulate from developing the family business, I will establish a venture capital arm that supports local promising entrepreneurs. My experience with a Lebanese business incubator showed me that there exists a critical divergence between the incredible amount of entrepreneurial talents in Lebanon and the lack of funding and advisory services to support them. By investing 'smart' and 'patient' capital in high-impact enterprises, the venture capital arm will play a pivotal role in creating economic opportunities in Lebanon and the region.

Wharton's MBA program with its leadership edge will help me achieve my career aspirations. The Entrepreneurial Management major and hands-on elective courses such as 'Strategies and Practices of Family-Controlled Companies' and 'Venture Capital and the Finance of Innovation' will provide me with the tools and experiences to run and modernize my family business and contribute to my region's development.

Emerging Markets and Latin America

I hope to make leveraged finance in Latin America the focus of my career. The field is appealing to me because I find that projects in sub-investment grade economies have more potential to significantly improve living standards of the general population. Having grown up in many global environments, I hope to bridge my experiences to international business. After graduating from business school, I plan to work long-term in Latin America.

For this reason, Wharton's noteworthy Lauder Program is the best match for my needs. Focusing on business level Spanish classes, international management, and study abroad programs, is an excellent way for me to gain the crucial foundational building blocks that are essential to the development of an effective international business leader.

However, I am not simply interested in the broad field of international business. I am drawn to the Emerging Markets because I see enormous potential in developing countries. For example, a strong argument suggests that a decoupling effect has developed among BRIC countries, which demonstrates BRIC independence from the influential US economy. This growth is likely to continue as foreign investment accelerates.

Over the past several years, I have also developed a keen interest in Microfinance in Latin America. I have participated in several microfinance organizations, and am now in the beginning stages of registering a Latin American microfinance non-profit.

Wharton's finance instruction, networking opportunities, and international focus stand to enhance the skill sets I have acquired over the past four years of my professional life in finance. With a solid foundation from my studies at Wharton, my goal is to focus on the area of the world economy that has the greatest need, the Emerging Markets.

Focused on Customer Analytics

Traditional marketers rely primarily on their intuition when deciding how to promote their products. However, in the advent of interactive marketing, my objective is to drive consumer demand at a multinational technology firm—such as Apple or Google—through quantitative analysis. I would begin in the consumer insights group, moving up to a marketing executive position. I want to lead a technology company to the cutting-edge of marketing, as firms in this dynamic industry must constantly find new ways to market their products. Such a career path would be especially rewarding because it would combine my creative and quantitative interests with my international background.

Working in marketing analytics consulting proved a natural progression from my econometrics training and advertising internships in Sofia and London. I mastered direct marketing by helping technology clients understand their business customers and increase return on marketing investment to over 300%. What I learn through Wharton's Interactive Media Initiative courses will further prepare me for the modern challenges of marketing. I would like to put these skills into practice by promoting social events for the *Europa*! club and leading my future company into successfully adopting the latest marketing innovations.

Articles in *Ad Age* and a *FastForward* webinar with Professor David Reibstein sparked my interest in becoming a CMO when I learned that the traditionally creative role is increasingly quantitative. I also spoke with the CMO of Hallmark, a Colgate alum, who confirmed her diversity of responsibilities—from working on sales forecasts with the customer insights department to reviewing creatives with the agency. While my marketing analytics experience would help me find a job in industry, Wharton's Business Fundamentals core curriculum would enable me to achieve my professional objective of creating innovating marketing by improving my understanding of how marketing interacts with other parts of the company.

How Wharton Can Help Healthcare

In the long term, I aim to manage my own business in the health care services sector, focusing on developing elder care in Brazil, a country with a booming economy and precarious public health systems. The Brazilian over-65 population is projected to increase seven times by 2050 and elder care is practically nonexistent. My mid-term goal is to establish a chain of geriatric care centers of superior quality, providing the elderly with daily medical service, comfortable facilities and diversified routine activities. Currently, I'm finishing a business plan to start a day care clinic, offering a reliable daily health care alternative for families' aging relatives. With help from my family this pilot will be implemented in 2011. After the MBA, I will take the lead to expand it to the geriatric chain.

The MBA at Wharton will help me achieve these goals, providing the education I need to improve as a manager, leader and entrepreneur. I have dedicated my career thus far to business, to later contribute to my family's health care company. At McBain, I developed my analytical skills and an integrated, broad sense of business. At Whirlpool I experienced the challenges of managing in a large leading corporation. To differentiate myself, I improved my communication and even self-promotion skills. At Wharton, I plan to develop my posture as a leader and gain exposure to new ways of thinking about strategy and finance. I'll take the **"Decision Models and Uncertainty" and "Innovation, Change & Entrepreneurship" courses and the Health Care Field Application Project.** Participating in clubs such as the Wharton Global Health Volunteers, I'll create a strong network, learning from diverse experiences and leadership styles. Finally, through a summer job at a leading health care company, I'll put theory into practice to further manage a business in the area.

▶ EDITOR'S NOTE

A recurring theme throughout these essays is whether to answer the question explicitly or what you *think* is being asked. This applicant did a great job weaving in her ambitions with how Wharton would specifically help. It is not mandatory but is done to great effect in this essay.

From Family to Career

I see my career as a materialization of my personal aspirations through activities I appreciate. In this sense, a desire to contribute to society and an interest in business has shaped my professional objective: in the future I want to become an international business leader who combines financial success with positive social impact. I see myself some years from now leading a global institution like World Bank, whose mandate combines elements of the business world with social impact, or a multinational company like PepsiCo, which, under the leadership of the ex-McBainer Indra Nooyi, works towards the goal of "performance with purpose".

From an early age I developed an interest for business. Through my father, an entrepreneur, I saw how exciting and rewarding, albeit challenging, business could be. Since then I have focused my studies and career in management: I pursued a business degree at university and started working at McBain, where I have had the opportunity of gaining strategy and management skills for almost three years now.

My interest for social impact activities also has origins in my family. By helping my grandparents to take care of poor children and elderly citizens during summer holidays I started to work for the community. Today I have a more consistent social impact activity, although having an unpredictable and minimal bandwidth for extra-McBain activities. My role as advisor at an NGO that provides after-school activities for children in a slum in Sao Paulo, allows me to combine my management skills with social impact. After professionalizing their management practices in 2009, I have been advising its investment and funding decisions to guarantee the wellbeing of the 250 children we take care of. As one of the other smaller social activities I also take part, I am now organizing *Projeto Sol's* golf day with my family, an event in which we will receive all our friends and business contacts, including presidents of big multinationals, for golf and fun, while offering them the opportunity of contributing to *Projeto Sol*. I am sure it will be a success and the first of a series.

The combination of business and social impact is not only a pleasant choice for me. Companies today can be responsible for groups of people sometimes larger than those found in entire cities or even small nations. Because of this, I do believe companies have a great and quite untapped potential to shape a better society, and I want to be prepared by Wharton-Lauder to be part of the leading team that will bring this potential to reality.

Progressive Investing

At Venture Partners we invest in for-profit social enterprises that are profitable, but that also reinvest part of their proceeds into the community. I intend to pursue this passion: first as an investor and later an entrepreneur, I will build a successful portfolio of social enterprises that will dominate their markets, out-competing their for-profit competitors. To achieve this, I will combine two necessary pieces of the puzzle: financial/business analysis skills, and important entrepreneurial qualities.

My career to-date has provided me the first piece of the puzzle. Working at one of the most successful investment banks in the world, I have gained an outstanding set of financial structuring and analysis skills across a range of financial products. My intimate involvement in the founding of the Financial Sponsors Group entrusted me with responsibilities well above the level of a typical analyst. At Venture Partners, I have honed my business/market analysis skills, and gained exposure to the social enterprise model in its many forms.

An MBA from Wharton will provide me with the missing piece of the puzzle. I will develop the well-rounded management skill set and influential network I require. With such a vast array of course options and program alternatives, Wharton is the perfect place to achieve my goal. Courses such as "Entrepreneurship and Venture Initiation" as well as "Societal Wealth Venturing" will enable me to enhance my skill set and achieve my professional objectives. Moreover, Wharton's reputation for student-run activities is a major attraction, and I hope to help lead clubs such as "Social Impact (WSI)" and the "Entrepreneurship Club".

My immediate post-MBA path will see me work at an 'impact investment' firm such as Bridges, where I will work on a wide a range of investments in for-profit social enterprises. Armed with this experience, I will later go on and found my own social enterprise, with the aim of one day taking it public, creating the first quoted social enterprise in the world.

From Domestic to International Banker

While at the Bank, I often found myself on the defensive at social events, Penn reunions and family gatherings: I did not trade or structure subprime mortgages nor did I "convince" people to take on loans they couldn't possibly afford! During my four years at the Bank I helped international investors become comfortable investing in Peru's electrical infrastructure. I helped a Mexican company hit hard by the drop-off in tourism, issue a bond in the international markets to refinance near-term maturities and help ensure the solvency of the company as a going concern. I am proud of my work, the people I have met and the lessons I have learned. I have worked with exciting companies in Chile, Brazil, Mexico and Peru. Through my work I have seen how business is conducted during a cross-border transaction in an increasingly global environment, and the potential of inefficiencies as a result of cultural misunderstandings.

I hope that by getting my MBA from Wharton I will be able to develop strategies for tackling a wide range of business challenges (including cultural issues) and then apply a broader strategic vision in a real-world business setting. Upon graduation I will move to Latin America and use what I have learned and the network of people I have met at the Bank and Wharton to ultimately help businesses grow in Latin America and expand internationally. I want the insights of others who have embarked on similar projects, the advice of my motivated classmates in my cohort and clubs; and the guidance of professors (such as Michael Useem) and alumni to further develop many of the skills I already have. I want to develop the right strategies and recruit the right people to make my vision real and as a result play a key role in facilitating Latin America's growth and prosperity, eventually leading to further social development. That is my professional objective and I hope you give me the opportunity to discuss it further with you.

Strategic Advice for Impact

My ultimate career aspiration is to become a catalyst for proliferation of profit-generating social enterprises. Born in Korea, raised in Thailand and educated in the U.S., I was exposed to social inequalities early. On the backdrop of high-rise skyscrapers in downtown Bangkok, bare-footed young children clung onto windows of my father's Mercedes sedan, begging for money. I offered direct assistance to underprivileged by partaking in non-profit organizations such as *Habitat for Humanity* to fight social imbalance, only to realize the limitation of such approaches. These people needed fundamental assistance to become self-sufficient. But *how?*

I found my answer when I fortuitously picked up '*Bankers for the poor*' by Muhammad Yunus in my junior year in college. Social enterprise, which makes profit while solving pressing social issues, was exactly what I had been looking for. With the success stories like Grameen-Danone JV in Bangladesh, Corporate Social Responsibility (CSR) is no longer considered as a mere corporate marketing tool in disguise but a real value-creating strategy for many corporations. By producing nutrient-rich children's yogurt at a lower cost, Danone helped to relieve Bangladeshi children of malnutrition, and create hundreds of jobs in local factory and farms. At the same time, Danone learned valuable lessons in manufacturing for the developing countries and even for business in the West.

The past three years at McBain has inspired and shaped my aspiration to dedicate myself to the development of CSR in Korean companies. Although Korea is still nascent in the area of CSR, my interactions with the top managements of Korean conglomerates demonstrated their growing interests in CSR. Given management consultant's influence over their decisions, I saw an opportunity to create not one, but hundreds of social enterprises like Grameen-Danone JV by providing professional advisory services to these conglomerates.

After Wharton, as a recipient of McBain MBA sponsorship, I would return to McBain to establish corporate social responsibility practice to provide socially-responsible business models and strategies to companies looking to improve their CSR. Upon their success, I would branch out to create my own social ventures. The thought of making lasting impacts to global society inspires me.

Innovative Hybrid Business Models

During my three years in Mexico, I have witnessed a cultural defect with implications so powerful it may be the reason most of the country is still trapped in the third-world. Whereas many Americans are attentive to helping those less fortunate, in Mexico, most people don't subscribe to this notion. Mexico represents a classic case in which the rich get richer at the expense of the poor getting poorer. This is a situation that undoubtedly exacerbates, if not causes, the drug wars, destitution in rural farming communities and glaring gaps in education that are severely inhibiting Mexico's economic development.

I aspire to play an active role in changing Mexico's society by establishing a profit-generating social enterprise in Mexico that will begin to bridge the cultural classist divide. I am particularly interested in a hybrid business model, similar to that of TOMS Shoes. TOMS uses a "one-for-one" concept: for every pair of shoes purchased, a pair of shoes is given to a child in desperate need in a poor community abroad. This business model is interesting because it doesn't rely on charity to bring about positive change in the community, but is still able to generate a profit.

During my time at Wharton, I will seek out innovative business ideas attractive to the segment of Mexicans who don't participate in Habitat for Humanity but purchase hundreds of dollars in Christmas gifts through UNICEF. I believe this hybrid model would have potential to expand and adapt to other countries, particularly Brazil, to break down socio-economic barriers in other communities with stalled economic development. I hope to eventually have a presence in all of Latin America, while continuing my career as a successful businesswoman and being a role model to young women in Latin America.

Merging the Private and Public Sectors

I aim to lead an organization that measurably improves the chances of disadvantaged populations across the United States. In advising thriving corporations at McBain and outstanding foundations and nonprofits at Bridgespan, I have learned that the rigorous, analytic approach of the private sector can help solve our nation's toughest problems. Bringing this experience to bear on the social sector to tackle economic inequality will be very powerful.

Working with top managers and investors I have learned that strong leadership and strategic thinking differentiate double-digit growth from dismal performance. An MBA, followed by operational experience at a global corporation, will enhance my leadership abilities and complete my skills. I will be well-placed to bring an analytic and strategic approach to the social sector. My goal is to lead an organization like Bridgespan or the Edna McConnell Clark foundation (whose investments in high-performance nonprofits I admire). Once established, I will draw on my international background to bring the skills of nonprofit and philanthropic foundations internationally.

I was raised in a diverse neighborhood of New York City and witnessed the effects of inequality first-hand. Success was often based on access to resources and not merit or hard work. As the leader of an organization in the social sector, I intend to change opportunities in disadvantaged communities and increase chances for success.

I view an MBA as critical in realizing my full potential as a manager and advisor. I am confident that Wharton's rigorous approach to problem-solving, diversity of students, and opportunities in consulting and the social sector, is the ideal platform from which to achieve my goals. I have seen my impact with nonprofits magnified by advancing my private sector skills. Wharton will continue this development and prepare me to lead an innovative organization that increases opportunities for the underserved.

From Space to the Cirque du Soleil

My professional progress covers nine years and has transformed a young MIT graduate into the founding owner and GM of a small Cirque du Soleil-style event management company. Along the way, I worked at the MIT Space Plasma Group, studied at the Ecole Nationale de Cirque in Montreal, researched at a Mayo Clinic neurology lab, produced my own circus tours through Europe, managed part of a multi-million-dollar project in Japan, and produced, created, and toured the first-ever Asian-produced cirque-nouveau show, "FLASH." Each seemingly unrelated step along the path is tied together by my underlying curiosity and desire to pursue ever-larger challenges; each step has contributed to a valuable skills base for a career producing events for clients in the Netherlands, Turkey, the United Arab Emirates, India, Thailand, Vietnam, Cambodia, Taiwan, Korea, Japan, the United States, and Canada. Now, the timing is right for me to pursue the Wharton MBA, a career cornerstone that is critical to 1) my short-term goal of applying my real-world experience to a formal business education, 2) my long-term career goal of applying that ability and my entrepreneurial instinct to an international consulting career for entrepreneurial business in Asia, and 3) an ultimate goal of making global, international business opportunities more available to entrepreneurs in countries with adverse financial or social conditions.

My university years were marked by left-brain/right-brain conflict. On the one hand, the quantitative skill set that I acquired at MIT and later developed as an MIT and Mayo Clinic researcher is a valuable business tool, but, on the other hand, after graduation, I still had professional ambitions as an acrobatic performer. Despite a career in space research, I decided to take a leap of faith by auditioning for the Cirque du Soleil partner school, l'Ecole Nationale de Cirque, despite being far older than the average student, having just recovered from a career-threatening injury, and not speaking a word of French. The audition process, I reasoned, in which more than 1000 international students vie for just 15 places, would be a turning point in my life. If I was accepted, I would overcome all such obstacles and absorb everything that the school had to offer.

Ultimately, the superficially "useless" experience of circus school has in fact provided a valuable business edge. Beyond professional credibility, the education provided a network spanning a who's-who in entertainment. This has helped me sell to initially hesitant Asian clients on many occasions. At circus school, as part of a close-knit group of 20 students from five countries, I also learned valuable lessons in interpersonal and international skills. We literally held each other's lives in our hands every day – practical leadership and team-building work, indeed – and learned that the social network of an industry is as important as any technical or theoretical know-how.

The weight that my MIT diploma carries abroad and that my Ecole Nationale de Cirque diploma carries within the industry has opened doors to the upper management offices of Cirque du Soleil, Dentsu Tec, Toho Geino, the National Theatre of Taiwan, the Vietnamese Ministry of Culture, Hillside Leisure Group in Turkey, the municipal offices of Yokohama, Japan and Yilan County, Taiwan, the New National Theatre of Tokyo, Feld Entertainment, the Guthrie Theatre, Hakuhodo, Inc, the Japanese Agency for Cultural affairs, and former Japanese Prime Minister, Tsutomu Hata. In two years of practical experience in development and successful productions with Jerry Snell Industries, I had built a large enough client base to incorporate my own company, New Circus Asia.

I know that a Wharton MBA degree will not do my business for me – doors never open without the audacity and initiative to knock on them in the first place – but I hope that it will be a sort of "brain" for the "guts" and the instinct that I have developed on-the-fly in the real world. A degree is no substitute for field-proven personal skills, courage, risk-taking and a die-hard refusal to fail.

New Circus Asia is a small, mobile, competitive, events-managing company. We provide advanced levels of service to both client and hired artists and offer attention-to-detail in production value to exceed client expectations. Years of practical experience in international entertainment affords me a level of comfort and authority that puts my client at ease. Despite New Circus Asia's success, my short-term goals have turned towards leaving the company to pursue a Wharton MBA. I have assembled a manage-ment staff of five and have been preparing my repeat clients for the changeover by introducing staff in rotation as deputy project managers to showcase their international management skills and their grace under fire that has become my company's trademark.

New Circus Asia has taught me that my strongest points are my ability to navi-gate complicated East-West international situations, my multilingual interpersonal skills, and my quantitative science background which helps me find creative solutions to seemingly insurmountable obstacles. My long-term goal is thus to change industries and move into a wider field in which those strengths will figure greatly: that of inter-national business consulting.

At Wharton, I hope to integrate cross-cultural business sense and real-world experiences with formal business disciplines. I want to contribute to and benefit from a dynamic and passionate mix of globally-minded students. My goal is a major in Entrepreneurial Management and a minor Finance, but I plan to pursue every opportunity available through the school. For example, I'm interested in the work of Professor Peter Fader of the Wharton Media and Entertainment Initiative, particularly since the trend in live acrobatic entertainment is to tap film directors in creating new productions. I hope to join the Consulting Club, Entrepreneurship Club, International Development Club, and the Media and Entertainment Club to meet with like-minded students. My passion lies in international work, so the opportunity to immerse myself in the Lauder Institute program will serve both my long-term goal and my ultimate goal, which is to help provide entrepreneurial opportunities to all business people based on the merit of their ideas and not on their particular financial or social situations. A Wharton MBA is the cornerstone of these goals, and, with my company on the brink of autonomy, the timing couldn't be better.

Revolutionizing the Banking Sector and Financial Products

My professional objective is to rebuild trust and understanding of financial services and products among an increasingly global and economically diverse set of consumers. I aim to build the world's largest online bank and use technology to target a generation for whom the traditional banking model used by their parents is no longer suited to their life-style or values. Akin to Apple's revolutionary impact on electronics, I want consumers to not be intimidated and confused by pensions and mortgages but view them as helpful, easy to use and even cool!

I will initially use my MBA experience to join a startup online lending or payments firm such as wonga.com. Using this operational experience I hope to either start my own venture or join an existing startup to develop a more comprehensive online banking business model. The finance side of banking has seen significant innovation but lagging are ideas for engaging customers. Instead of increasing late fees and hidden charges I want to focus on creating profits through creative consumer driven solutions. For example, how can the psychology behind computer game design be used to help students more intuitively manage their finances? The next step would be to identify how these services can be broadened so their inherent benefits reach beyond one student to an entire country. Launching into markets such as India, Brazil or East Africa, where a meaningful banking offer could significantly improve social mobility and counter the concentration of wealth, would have tremendous short and long-term benefits, both locally and globally.

My experience at McBain and Technoserve has helped me develop many skills relevant to my career objective, but a Wharton MBA would provide unparalleled access to experts that could help me fully flesh out how I can make banking better at serving the needs of society.

TURNED DOWN OPPORTUNITIES

Reflect on a time when you turned down an opportunity. What was the thought process behind your decision? Would you make the same decision today? (600 words)

INTRODUCTION

Like most of the essays required when writing a business school application, the question of a time that you turned down an opportunity is hardly about the opportunity you turned down and more about what you did and why. It is almost entirely about your decision-making process. It is another opportunity for the admissions committee to gain insight into who you are, how you think, and what your priorities are. As such, do not worry about what specific opportunity you turned down, be it professional, personal, or other. Focus more on the reasons you made specific decisions in the context of your longer term plans and what really motivates you to succeed.

In the next pages, you will find some essays that might surprise you. Some of the decisions might seem inconsequential. For example, deciding between two great job opportunities is not the worst position to be in! Some might even seem selfish. For example, turning down the opportunity to work for a non-profit in favor of continuing a lucrative private sector job. Others are extremely moving, involving personal hardship and challenging family situations. What unites these essays and makes them successful is not the examples they use. It is a dedication to a specific cause and belief that shows tenacity in the face of adversity or opportunity. Similarly, it is the process of thinking through a decision and learning from the many choices that life can present.

In the paragraphs you have to discuss why you turned down an opportunity, do not be afraid to let your character shine through. Be it thoughtful, logical and plodding, or passionate and enthusiastic, the admissions committee will be far more likely to accept the application of a person they feel they "know" than simply a flat recounting of events that lacks color and authenticity. Above all, be sure to tie this essay into one of your main themes in your personal story and be genuine.

Turning Down the Presidency

In April of my sophomore year of college, my classmates elected me to be a Student Senator. I was then elected by the Student Senate to be a member of the University Council (now known as the University Senate) and by the 12 student members of the University Council to be the University Council Vice-Chair, the highest student position in the faculty-staff-student legislative body. At the time, those who followed the Student Senate widely considered me as the frontrunner to be the next student body president. But that did not happen – in fact, I never even stood for election.

The race for student body president at the university is all consuming for the candidates, and, during the summer before my junior year, I made the fatal error of diverting my attention away from the upcoming election. While I was busy recruiting rising freshman to join my fraternity, two other potential presidential candidates were busy recruiting student leaders to join their Student Senate coalitions. Once alerted, I was able to consolidate much of what I had anticipated would be my base of support, but by that time my would-be opponents had crossed the Rubicon. Despite my best efforts, they would not be dissuaded from running.

I faced what I now know to be one of the more important decisions I have ever had to make: whether to put my name on the ballot to possibly achieve a goal I set at freshman orientation. I already had enlisted an eminently likeable, highly influential colleague in the Student Senate to join the ticket as my vice presidential running mate, and together we successfully had convinced a diverse array of involved students to join our team. I also knew that I could draw on the knowledge and experience of the three previous student body presidents, each of whom had pledged his support to my candidacy. But the emergence of not one but two formidable opponents meant the six-plus month campaign would not only be expensive and time-intensive but also incredibly close. I remained confident that I could – and would – win if I ran a strong campaign, but I realized that the pole position I once occupied had been lost during those summer months. The prospect of being subjected to negative campaigning tipped the balance, and, despite the progress that I had made in forming a coalition to support my candidacy, I ultimately declined to run.

I count the decision to bow out of the race to be among my best ever. As disappointed as I was at the time, I used my departure from the race as a springboard from which to achieve more significant goals. Much of the time I would have otherwise spent campaigning I used to concentrate on my studies, and to great effect: my GPA improved from a 3.46 during my first two years to a 3.84 during my last one and a half. In the ensuing months and years, I took part in a summer study abroad program, traveled across Europe, graduated a semester early and moved to and worked in London following graduation, none of which I could have accomplished had I stayed in the race. Faced with the same choice today, I would not have to think twice before proceeding exactly as I did then.

The Road Less Traveled

As a child, I was fascinated by the world of intelligence. Perhaps it was the 70's era James Bond movies I watched growing up and wishing my parents' car could shoot rockets like Sean Connery's. At Georgetown, I took every intelligence-related class I could get into, even begging professors to let me audit their graduate-level classes for no credit, because I found the material so interesting.

Naturally, when I joined the military, I requested to be an intelligence officer; however, there were no intelligence positions available when I applied. Instead, my 20/20 eyesight and military aptitude scores made me eligible for pilot training. I was disappointed, but becoming an officer was more important to me than any specific occupation I would be trained in.

Less than a month before flight school began, my instructor came to me with an opportunity: Marines who had been slated to become pilots could now change their occupational specialty to something else. Here was the opportunity that I had wanted - I could now become an intelligence officer, part of that glamorous world I had dreamed of. I filled out the requisite paperwork, and slept fitfully that night. A few days later, I was ordered to meet with the school's deputy commander.

After an agonizing wait on the secretary's couch, I was called into the colonel's office. As I snapped to attention in front of the enormous desk, my eyes drifted from the colonel's pilot wings on his chest to the wall of photographs behind him, shaking hands with US presidents in front of the executive White House helicopter. "Tell me, Lieutenant, why do you want to be an intelligence officer?" the colonel asked. I delivered my carefully reasoned argument, mentioning my academic background in intelligence and my passion for the industry. "Very well", he said, unemotionally. "Here are your reassignment papers. But before I sign, you owe it to yourself to answer this question: One day, when you are old with grandchildren on your lap, how will you feel telling them the story about how you ALMOST became a pilot?" His words still ringing in my head, he handed me the papers gave me until the end of the week to reconsider. If I still wanted intelligence, he would sign off, no questions asked.

I wrestled with the decision all week, and talked to many pilots and intelligence officers to get their perspectives. While there was no clear path, it became clear that intelligence was actually a "safe" choice - despite the excitement of James Bond movies, most officers really spent their time in staff offices, not in operations. Aviation was much more unpredictable and risky – I would be deployed in combat zones and finish my contract at the age of 30. The advantage of intelligence was that I would finish my contract at 26, better positioned for a post-military MBA. Despite these advantages, the week came and went. I decided not to pursue the intelligence option after all – instead, I chose to be a pilot.

When I look back on my life, I realize my most satisfying decisions are the ones that have taken me out of my comfort zone and into a personal challenge: studying in a foreign country, becoming a motorcycle rider, joining the military. I have no regrets about turning down the opportunity to be an intelligence officer, and I would make the same decision today. I frequently remind myself of Robert Frost's words "I took the one less traveled, and that has made all the difference."

Business and Creative Arts

To Bollywood or McBain? After graduating with a seemingly clear future and a dream job as an associate with McBain, I chose to spend my last summer vacation studying acting at Mumbai's premier institute, driven by a childhood fascination. With help from serendipity and my mother's childhood friend, I was offered a supporting role in a major film featuring some of India's leading stars: *Dus Kahaniyan.*

Growing up, my artistic hobbies ranged from Indian music to dance. In 2006, I won Michigan's inaugural university-wide music competition and a record deal with a Bollywood-inspired song and traveled to Mumbai to sell my record. However, raised in a traditional Indian home, I'd never seriously considered a career in entertainment.

The McBain offer, on the other hand, was the ideal first step to a career in business. I'd grown up in a business atmosphere: my grandfather ran an airline, my uncle took one of his three companies public, and my mother heads a mid-sized IT-staffing firm. After exploring other fields in college, I zeroed in on a BBA myself, choosing McBain for the insight I'd have into the workings of leading companies' executive teams.

The decision tore at me for weeks. My first reactions were emotional. I had glamorous visions of what the role would bring. But just as quickly, I felt a stab of guilt as I had committed to start with McBain in a month. I set out to get the facts. Discussing the script and role with Mr. Deol, I determined that while the role was not insignificant, it was no guarantee of a career. With little acting training, sustaining a livelihood afterwards was going to be a challenge. On the McBain front, I called my hiring principal, and he was unequivocal; I was 50% of the starting class in the nascent Detroit office, and my start date could not be postponed for the required three months. Reneging would hurt staffing plans, but staying for one year would give them a chance to adjust hiring the next recruiting season.

With the gravity of my commitment to McBain in mind, I analyzed the secondary aspects with my two closest advisors – my parents. Among many pros and cons discussed and documented, a central point kept recurring: entertainment was a fickle industry and required a strong backup plan. I had worked incredibly hard to get to the Ross School of Business and then to McBain to build the foundations for a career in business. Leaving that track now would make returning difficult: Jobs with firms like McBain were not easy to get, and would open many doors in the future.

Guided by my career and commitment, I turned down the opportunity. But I drew a timeline that kept open the option of pursuing an entertainment career a year later –

something I ended up doing in a more structured way, formally studying acting, dance, and screenwriting at the prestigious Lee Strasberg Institute in New York.

Looking back, I'm proud that I honored my commitment and would make the same decision today – though this seemed less clear when I shuffled into the theatre to watch the movie on a cold Michigan Friday, after a long week at McBain. Even knowing now, that a role that prominent never came my way again, it was the right decision for me. I discovered that my love for the entertainment industry is real, but realized the difficulty of building a career on the "creative side." I recognized that my personality and strengths are best suited for the more viable and secure "business side." Without McBain, I would not be in a position to pursue my dream of leading a media company, and likely would not have had the lens to see the industry's potential and envision that dream had I not experienced strategy's power to shape the future.

Turning Down a Great University

My undergraduate studies at the American University of Beirut (AUB) made me realize the great passion I had for economics. From my first class to my final econometrics paper, I truly enjoyed each and every economics course I took. At the end of my senior year, I had the opportunity to further pursue this passion through a Masters degree at the London School of Economics. I decided, however, to decline the opportunity.

A few weeks before receiving an acceptance from LSE, I was extended an offer to join (McBain) in Dubai. Prior to my senior year, the idea of working right after college had never crossed my mind. However, after being introduced to management consulting, and to McBain more particularly, it wasn't hard for me to envision myself as a consultant. What I liked most about the industry was the great learning opportunities it offered to fresh graduates. I was impressed to see how, within few years of experience, young consultants were able to develop very concrete business skills, making it possible for them to have an impact on the region. At first, it seemed as if I had to choose between my passion for economics and an interesting job opportunity. However, my previous experiences had shown me that I simply cannot excel and be happy when I am not pursuing my passions. I was about to accept LSE's offer when I realized that McBain was not just an interesting job.

Back then, I was a Red Cross manager and my team and I were helping the students of an underprivileged school in Beirut. Twice per week and for six months, we were giving tutoring sessions to fifty students. In addition, we were organizing arts, theater and social education classes that the school could not afford to offer. When the school principal told me how impressed the teachers were by the attitude and results of the students we were helping, I realized that, beyond economics, what I was really passionate about was making a difference in people's lives. In other words, the reason I loved economics was not only because it helped me understand how the world works, but mostly because it showed me how I can shape it. From that angle, I saw McBain's offer differently. Becoming a consultant was more than a great learning experience; it was another way for me to achieve my passion: helping others and contributing to the development of my country and region.

My Red Cross experience also made me realize that I enjoyed working with people and driving change on the ground rather than from an office. Seeing my work and efforts affecting others was far more important to me than writing a great economic paper and never seeing it implemented. During my internship with the International Labor Organization, I was in charge of identifying which institutions in Lebanon supported the reconstruction efforts after the 2006 war. One of the insights I took away from this experience was how the abundance of research entities contrasted with the limited number of organizations capable of implementing all their great recommendations. I knew then that LSE might provide me with the intellectual stimulation I loved, but it would not give me the tools to help others and shape the world: I was a 'doer' more than a scholar. And just like that, my signature was printed on McBain's job offer.

Three years later, I can confidently say that I made the right choice. McBain provided me with invaluable experiences and tools that LSE could simply not offer. Using these tools, I may not have changed the world yet, but I've certainly helped others, be it Berytech's entrepreneurs, NGOs such as the Industrial Research Institute or my family business.

Goodbye Law, Hello Rome

In 2003 I was in the 4th year of Law School in Sao Paulo. I was working for one of the largest law firms in Brazil with renowned lawyers as bosses and in the field I appreciate the most, Corporate Law. Workload was overwhelming and many times after university classes in the evening, I would return to the office to finish some work, do research or prepare myself for next day meetings. I was only 21 years old and already had a clear ambition, to succeed in my career.

Even with a tight schedule, to me it was absolute pleasure to wake up at 5.30am twice a week to attend Italian classes. Among all languages I had learned, Italian has always been my favorite as I developed a special appreciation for the Italian culture. My dedication was recognized as I was indicated to be sponsored to finish my studies in Rome.

The only 'but' was that to accept the scholarship I would have to quit my internship and interrupt Law School for at least one year. My boss at the time guaranteed me a job position after graduation if I decided to stay. Colleagues and family considered it a "no-brainer" decision. It was a really promising job offer. However, to me, it was not only about accepting or turning down a scholarship. It was about searching for my personal growth and feeding my cultural curiosity. It was an opportunity to get in touch with a different culture, to live among Romans and to share the classroom with other international students.

I was aware of the risks. This decision could influence future recruiters and not be well perceived. I could come back to Brazil and struggle to find a job as good as the one I was leaving. But I was sure that the experience would enrich me as a person and, by consequence, could make me a better professional. So I turned down the job offer, accepted the scholarship.

The experience exceeded my expectations. After only 3 months studying and living in Rome, I passed the Italian proficiency test. My goal had been reached. I had become a more educated person as I'd lived the Italian lifestyle, explored the arts, learned the traditions and mastered the language. I then longed to experience the most cosmopolitan European city, so I bought a ticket to London. During my 7-month stay I worked as hostess of a restaurant and as waitress at a local pub. To work in a different country performing such diverse tasks made me develop maturity to deal with all sorts of adverse situations. I was more self-aware of my abilities and realized that for my upcoming professional life I would not only rely on my brains, but also on the soft skills I had gained. Before coming back to Brazil I decided to backpack Europe which opened my mind to different realities and to teachings of cross-cultural experiences. One year later, I married my French spouse in Brazil and my sensitivity to cultures differences helped us overcome the language and social obstacles.

Three months after my arrival in Brazil I was selected as one of the 20 trainees at Itau (among more than 1,500 candidates) and at the end of the program it was up to me to decide whether to accept a position on the Legal Department or as a derivatives trader. I'm sure I made the right decision back in 2003 because I was ready to change careers. As a consequence of turning down that job offer, I went through a personal journey that gave me confidence to take risks and to always aspire to the best. And that one decision ultimately led me to pursuing a Wharton MBA degree, seeking my personal and professional development.

Focusing One's Efforts

In 2008, Universidade de São Paulo (USP) invited me to resume the course in international relations I had left three years before. I was given the chance to study two more years and obtain a degree in a subject I found fascinating. If I refused the offer, I would no longer be able to resume the course from where I had left off and would essentially be forgoing the chance to obtain a degree in this subject.

Aligned with my ambition of becoming an international business leader, in 2004 I started two undergraduate courses at the same time: one in business at Fundação Getúlio Vargas (GV) and another in international relations at USP. In 2006, however, I made the difficult decision of giving up the international relations degree. Having to start a mandatory internship for each degree, I did not have time for two jobs in addition to two sets of classes. While I enjoyed the coursework in international relations, a more business-focused career offered dynamic opportunities and better training. I saw my business school colleagues doing interesting work at banks and consulting firms and making good money whereas my colleagues in international relations were working for free as assistants of assistants in miscellaneous government offices.

By giving up international relations and continuing the business degree, I was able to work as an intern at the sales team of Banco Santander and as a consultant at Consulting Associates. Also, right after graduation I started to work as an associate at my current employer, (McBain), where I have had the opportunity of working in strategy cases in diverse industries, from chemicals to pharmaceutical to financial services.

The opportunity to resume the course in international relations came one year into my time at McBain. I was very tempted to turn back to texts and discussions about the global political economy. I was also excited by the possibility of attending lectures by ambassadors from different countries and by domestic leaders that represented Brazil in front of important international institutions such as the World Trade Organization, the International Labor Organization and the American Chamber of Commerce.

Despite the allure, I was acutely aware of my current constraints. Unpredictability and long hours – two pillars of a consultant's life – would mean I could not fully dedicate myself to the coursework or even guarantee that I would be able to attend classes. Attempting to navigate the situation, I even asked McBain whether it could guarantee my staffing in São Paulo, but it could not. Given these factors, I turned down the opportunity for good.

From that decision I understood that to pursue my objectives I will always have to make tradeoffs and prioritize. I learned to be creative and explore realistic paths to pursue my interests. Determined to make my career as international as possible, in my two and a half years of McBain I managed to work in three different countries and with several international groups – a unique accomplishment amongst my associate class. I also learned to look for new opportunities such as the Wharton-Lauder dual degree, in which I will be able to pursue international relations without giving up my business focus and career progression.

Because of all I learned, if I were to make the same decision today, I would be even more certain in keeping the position I had two years ago. Now I know that I am capable of leveraging all the different possibilities the world offers to generate gains that compensate or even surmount losses from the foregone opportunity.

Taking a Risk to Pursue a Meaningful Goal

Attending the United World College of the Atlantic changed my life. With 350 students from over 80 different countries, Atlantic College aims to make "education a force to unite people, nations and cultures for peace and a sustainable future". When I arrived at Atlantic College I was a 15-year old kid unaware of global affairs, but by the time I left I was a politically aware young adult who wanted to make a difference in the world. Atlantic College had exposed the injustices and inefficiencies of our world and I was determined to do something about it.

Fairly early on in my university days I decided that the best way for me to do this was through business. So recognising that I first needed the best business and financial training possible, I successfully pursued what I intended to be a temporary position in investment banking.

Fast forward three years, and I was part of a great team at a bank, with great colleagues, enjoyed a lot of senior support and was entrusted with an unusually high level of responsibility for someone in my position. I had just been promoted half a year early, and was already enjoying the opportunity of presenting to clients, something almost unheard of for someone of my level. My career at the bank looked extremely promising, and leaving did not seem a sensible option. But deep down I knew that investment banking was not where I had set out to be, and so I began investigating what my potential 'next step' could be. When I stumbled across Bridges I immediately fell in love with the institution. A pioneer in the 'impact investing' field, Bridges is a unique and promising type of venture capital fund, with only a select number of counterparts in other parts of the world, such as the Acumen Fund. Through its innovative investment approach, Bridges aims to show that attractive financial returns can be delivered successfully alongside social and/or environmental returns. Bridges was an extremely attractive proposition and so I applied for a position.

I soon discovered however that due to headcount restrictions Bridges could only offer me a place on their summer internship program. I was faced with a very tough decision. I was already unsure about turning down the opportunity of a successful career at the bank, but by accepting Bridges' internship offer I was also sacrificing my job security. After three years in which I had survived multiple job-cutting rounds and seen many of my friends made redundant and struggle to get back into the workforce, I knew this was a huge risk. But in the end I decided that I needed to do what I felt was right, and decided to accept Bridges' offer.

Joining Bridges is by far one of the best decisions I've ever made. At Bridges, I feel more professionally and personally satisfied than ever. I've worked first-hand on investments such as that in Babington College or in Whelan Refining that are helping to bring economic regeneration and stimulate investment in clean technology. My work is making a positive impact. My involvement in the potential investment in Venture 4 Life, a social enterprise which provides out-of-school education to permanently excluded students, has also shown me that financially profitable business models can be developed around social causes. Bridges has therefore given me a blueprint of my future career and shown me a way of carrying out my ambition to make a positive impact through business. Turning down the opportunity of a successful career at the bank to join Bridges is therefore one of the best decisions I've ever made, and I would happily make the same decision today.

Staying True to a Lifelong Passion

Last year I was offered the opportunity to work in the Bank's Leveraged Finance team. I politely turned them down so that I could continue with my focusing on Latin America, which remains my primary interest. At the Bank we have a Latin American group that is separate from its US counterparts and divided by the three product groups, Latam Mergers & Acquisitions (M&A), Latam Equity Capital Markets (ECM) and Latam Debt Capital Markets (DCM). For the last three years and during the peak of the credit crisis, I have worked in the Latam DCM team where I have helping corporations in Latin America both big and small raise financing in the international or their local capital markets. I have also helped certain corporations restructure their existing liabilities when their debt load exceeded their repayment capacity. Nevertheless the size and scope of some of these deals necessitated a broader deal team initiative that leveraged the expertise of the Leveraged Finance team dedicated to that area.

After one such transaction, a senior deal team member from the restructuring subgroup in Leveraged Finance, took me to coffee and offered me a position as part of his team. He mentioned that he was impressed with the initiative I had taken to successfully conclude a complex transaction for a Mexican manufacturer that had renegotiated existing obligations with creditors and subsequently looked for ways to reduce leverage. He stated that as part of his team I would gain more senior exposure in the bank as well as the opportunity to work on larger transactions with a greater degree of financial complexity. Though I appreciated the opportunity I declined his offer. My reason: everything I have done since high school has been guided by my interest in Latin America. My interest really took hold when I applied to the Huntsman Program at Wharton and naturally evolved when I joined the Bank's Latin American team.

I speak Spanish and English fluently. But I truly believe that more than any other Latin American that learns English or American that learns Spanish, I have a cultural background that allows me to relate easily to peoples of both cultures. I was born in Houston, Texas and grew up in Florida. However, my father's side of the family is from Argentina and my mother's is from Chile and I have often spent time visiting both sides of my family. I have lived my entire life by straddling lines of ethnic divides. In fact, the Senior Banker commented to me how comfortable he was working with me, knowing I would understand his expressions and ultimately his point of view. Likewise, clients are always relieved when I address them in Spanish, knowing that language will not be a hurdle in an upcoming transaction.

I did not tell the Senior Banker all my reasons when I politely declined his offer. I just thanked him for the coffee and told him I was happy where I was and that I would look forward to working with him on the next transaction. In high-school, when I was applying to the Huntsman Program I had a fair idea that anything I did down the line would relate in some way to my interest in Latin America. Now I know that whatever I do after receiving my MBA from Wharton will definitely relate to my interest in Latin America and will leverage my ability to help both people and businesses bridge cultural divides.

Unexpected Change and Choices

I landed at Incheon International Airport in January 2004 after graduating a semester early from Brown with a scholarship to a top U.S. graduate program in Economics, in line with my childhood dream of pursuing a PhD in academia. I was filled with high hopes to find workable solution to facilitate the proliferation of social enterprises utilizing the academic subject of my interest and arrived at my home country with excitement for a new beginning.

Situation at home, on the other hand, was not so rosy. My grim-parents greeted me at the airport and explained that our family's gemstone distribution business in Thailand went bankrupt, forcing the family to return to Korea without any assets. As the eldest son in a Korean family with both parents unemployed and a sister just accepted to college, it was expected that I would become the breadwinner. However, my decision to return to Korea to support my family was contingent upon serving two years in the Korean military, from which I was exempted due to my Thai resident status. The decision to relocate to Korea meant pushing back my life for a few years.

Despite the initial shock, I realized I had to make a choice. I was torn between taking up my duty as the eldest son as my parents had lost their vigor and the will to rebuild our family, and seizing the academic opportunity that I had worked hard to achieve. My decision had repercussions not only on my life but the lives of three others. Nothing in my life had prepared me to make a decision of such magnitude.

Through careful introspection of what is the right thing to do, I knew I could not abandon my family. Some might argue that with a more advanced degree I could have provided greater financial support later, or I could have started my professional career in the U.S. and to support my family financially from afar. But I felt that I needed to take a more direct route of facing the circumstances rather than to take a detached stance from overseas because I knew I needed to step up to be a leader of my family and to provide both financial and psychological support at that time of desperation. New opportunities would come later, I figured, but a chance to help my family may not. It was not an easy decision to make, but I learned that sometimes to do the right thing, I must be willing to give up the things that I desire the most, even my dreams.

I do not regret my decision to stay in Korea. Rather, I was blessed with rewarding outcomes that exceeded my expectations. Within the three years working at McBain, I had saved enough money to secure a small house for my family just outside of Seoul and see my sister graduate from college. My family overcame the danger of disintegration, got back on a more solid financial footing and, most importantly, cultivated a strong bond that had not existed in the years of abundance.

It was not easy – and it is *still* not easy. But I see the past five years of hardship, along with my experiences in the military, investment bank and consulting as a blessing in disguise. The sudden change in my family's economic status taught me to plan for a cause bigger than myself. Changing habitats and professions taught me to observe, listen and appreciate the multiplicity in answers and methods of attaining goals. These changes have shaped me to become a more mature, resilient and forward-looking person. I believe the lessons that I learned from my life's hardships will serve as guiding principles on my way to become a catalyst for proliferating profit-generating social enterprise in the future.

A Businesswoman in Mexico Over a Passion for Music

Recently, I was presented with a unique and exciting opportunity that lodged me between a rock and a hard place: work or passion? Should I take a 6-month leave of absence from McBain to develop the strategy for implementing a system of non-profit instrumental music education programs for underprivileged children in Mexico? To be modeled after "El Sistema" – the revolutionary Venezuelan social change music program – the program I envisioned would identify and target pilot communities, project funding requirements, identify sponsors and devise the implementation plan. Applying business strategy knowledge to the field of music for the benefit of society was something that married all of my interests so perfectly I was convinced it was destiny.

My initial reaction was to do it at all costs. It was the ideal way to get back into music – a passion I had put aside upon moving to Mexico, for lack of time and resources. The day I flawlessly performed my favorite Chopin nocturne at my senior recital marked the end of my 17-year career as a performing pianist. Now, I had a chance to revive this passion by bringing it to children who didn't have the means to experience the same empowering sensation. I wanted to be part of something revolutionary, and I believed this was it.

After the initial excitement wore off, I started thinking rationally and decided to turn down this opportunity. It was not a choice between work and passion; rather, it was a choice between two distinct passions. Though I believed in the cause, I had also fallen in love with solving strategic problems for globally-minded corporations. The thrill of being a young foreign female working alongside bigwig corporate executives in predominantly male environments rivaled the rush of performing for 400 people on a nine-foot concert grand piano.

This decision was not unlike many others I have had to make in the past. I applied the same three criteria as always: Is this something I will enjoy doing? Can I have a meaningful impact? Will this bring me closer to my long-term career goals?

Of course I would enjoy setting up music academies for children, working with the mastermind economist/musician behind "El Sistema." But I lacked connections to the movers and shakers, as they were deeply entrenched in Mexican bureaucracies to which I had no access. I didn't see any way to achieve critical milestones in such a short time without a full-time team. Furthermore, taking time out from McBain would have stalled my career growth at a crucial moment. I was coming up for promotion to Senior Associate Consultant and I didn't want to risk my promotion for something that would not generate results in time. Emotionally, turning down this opportunity was one of the most difficult decisions I ever had to make. Rationally, it couldn't have made more sense.

As I reflect on this decision six months later, I am convinced it was the right one. It was not aligned with my overall goals and could not provide me with significant new skills. I still needed structured professional guidance to become a successful consultant, something I would have struggled to obtain if I worked independently on this initiative. I would have foregone the chance to work on a project in Colombia and El Salvador – a long-awaited opportunity to do business outside of Mexico. As a direct result of my performance on that project, I was promoted, an accomplishment reserved for strong performers at McBain. Consequently, I am one step closer to having the resources to someday affect social change through other opportunities.

NAVIGATING A CHALLENGING EXPERIENCE

Discuss a time when you navigated a challenging experience in either a personal or professional relationship. (600 words)

INTRODUCTION

Navigating challenging situations is a common occurrence in the business world and is surprisingly frequent in business school, where networking, social events, and active club participation is de rigueur. The "Navigating a Challenging Experience" essay is an excellent way to demonstrate that you have encountered challenging experiences, be they in the workplace or personal life, and handled them with aplomb. Of course, the lessons you learned are always interesting to share with the reader.

This essay can be approached from a variety of angles. A challenging experience can simply be a large undertaking you have attacked with enthusiasm and succeeded at, namely a relatively standard accomplishment but one that took a lot of gusto. It can also, however, be a situation that did not go smoothly at first and a time when perhaps you did not immediately succeed with flying colors. These can be some of the most powerful demonstrations of success in the face of adversity.

As you will see in these successful essays, a great essay has a huge variety of possible angles. Many applications discuss relatively standard professional challenges such as older clients or assuming responsibilities outside of a defined role. This approach is perfectly acceptable as long as there was clear reflection and action taken. Be careful not to bore the reader! You will also see examples of college accomplishments and personal journeys, where the lessons learned and qualities demonstrated had very little to do with the usual hurdles professionals face at work.

From Legal Jockey to Business Advisor

"That's a business issue; we'll have to speak
with our client and get back to you."

I first heard a partner state this soon to become all-too-familiar negotiating refrain when I was participating in discussions for a $3.8 billion sale of Telesat Canada to a partnership formed by our client, the Public Sector Pension Investment Board. On that occasion, we were discussing the size and scope of the indemnification the seller would provide to the buying partnership, provisions that I understood to have significant implications on our client's revenue model. Throughout the course of our negotiations, both deal teams would repeat that mantra from time to time, most often because the resolution of an issue would have significant economic implications on the transaction. Although I entered the legal profession (perhaps naively) hoping that one day I would negotiate all of the deal terms, I came to learn that, as a general rule, lawyers are empowered to resolve only the legal points of an agreement while our clients hash out the primary business terms.

In a more recent transaction, I served as one of the primary negotiators for a client who is notorious among our firm's partners as being a micromanager. His interpretation of what constituted a "legal issue" was so narrow as to render me incapable of making any decisions without consulting him first. Although I received every indication from the supervising attorney that the client was confident in my abilities, I nonetheless had to recite the "business issue" mantra reserving final decisions on almost every issue, without respect to its nature or importance in the context of the deal. Apart from the frustration I felt as a result of having such limited discretionary authority, this dynamic ultimately posed a number of challenges to our relationship. After learning of agreements the client entered into independently with his business counterparties, I was compelled as a fiduciary to explain why certain compromises to which he agreed to were inadvisable if not altogether legally impermissible. I explained the problems as delicately as possible, but the client was nonetheless frustrated to learn that we needed to renegotiate certain items. And, although I was charged with finalizing the transaction agreements as quickly as possible, the process invariably stagnated as I had to negotiate with not just the other side's legal team but also my client.

Rather than dwelling on the decisions I was not authorized to make, I focused my energy on anticipating points of conflict with the other side that my client likely would insist on resolving at a business level. This approach ensured that my client received counsel even if I was not involved in every decision. I consulted with my colleagues and researched precedent transactions to determine what terms were considered "market" for similar deals and held anticipatory discussions with my client in order to educate him in case he reached agreements independently. I reviewed important court decisions and provided summaries thereof to my client to better equip him to protect his interests under the law. And, because of my actions, he gained a better appreciation of the scope of legal complexities of which he had been unaware. I also made it a point to always quantify potential liabilities in terms of dollar figures and percentages, an approach that demonstrated to my client that I did not analyze the transaction in the abstract but rather understood his primary focus. As a result, he began to insist that I be present for both the business and legal negotiations, and I found myself claiming that a point of contention was a "business issue" with ever-decreasing frequency.

Proving Value to an Older Client

I was leading my client team at McBain alongside a much older VP of Logistics, planning for the resulting logistical nightmare as a consumer-goods company consolidated five US plants to Mexico and neared bankruptcy. After forty years at the hierarchical company, he understandably had doubts about how my limited experience would bring value to the project. In an early meeting, he peppered me with industry-specific questions. I struggled to answer, trying to explain that I wasn't there for industry knowledge – I had McBain experts to that end – I was there to help them frame the issues, gather data, and do analysis. As I fumbled through an explanation far less eloquent, he cut me off to ask my age and the antagonistic tone for our working relationship was set.

My first strategy was to resolve the issue in person. I approached him afterwards, but was brushed aside. My problems doubled when my principal, leading the site selection team in Mexico, called to say the VP had expressed his lack of faith in me to the partner on the case. I was embarrassed.

My next strategy was to have a trusted third party vouch for me and address the VP's doubts, requesting my principal's vote of confidence and time to handle the situation. One of only two consultants at headquarters, I felt pressure to pull my own weight and deliver as the client quickly fell behind.

Although judged prematurely, I tried not to take it personally and remained respectful. My next strategy was direct email communication, to clarify my role and underline our common objective. When this went unanswered, I realized that it would take work, not words, to prove myself and earn his support. In one-on-one interviews with the team, I gathered information on shipping routes, logistics contracts, container costs, distribution centers, distances, and nuances of the five plants. But I found the team even less cooperative than before I'd publicly lost their boss's support.

My next strategy was to demonstrate maturity, meeting with the VP to discuss a theme I had noticed across the logistics, HR and legal teams: job security fears hampering productivity. Days later, I was surprised to see he had taken my input seriously – a CEO memo was distributed to the teams assuring job safety. I'd cracked his armor and won favor with the team.

But crucial time had passed and progress was near zero. My strategy for addressing his doubts about my experience was to dig deep into McBain's knowledge database and consult McBain experts. With the team's help, I spent weekends at the client-site and worked into the mornings to build the foundations of a logistics model that was the single piece of work I was most proud of at McBain. The model had an easy-to-use Visual Basic graphical interface, with buttons and geographic maps, and powerful capabilities to simulate numerous plant-shutdown and volume-shifting scenarios.

Warily eyeing the VP's "World's Best Grandpa" mug, I used my most effective strategy: demonstrating my value through my work. I sensed he was very impressed. My feeling was confirmed when he began to take ownership of the model. Employing my final strategy, I collaborated with him, using his seasoned input to make the model even more powerful, turning a seemingly intractable problem into easily simulated scenarios that could be manipulated by even a new user. Over the next few months, we built on our success, and our relationship turned extremely positive. The model became the central tool to plan and track the transition, and he directed questions to me, designating me the go-to person.

While trying strategies to work with the VP, fearful client-team members, and my remote McBain principal in a stressful environment, I learned the importance of finding ways to deliver, even when personalities clash. The successful move and subsequent McBain/client efforts cost US manufacturing jobs but saved a failing company: its share price, which had fallen to 60¢, now stands at $8.00 – proven value.

Gaining an Ally at the Ministry

Gaining the trust of a public servant with thirty-seven years of budgeting experience and using his support to change an organization is undoubtedly the most challenging yet rewarding professional experience I had at (McBain). In 2009, McBain supported a large Middle Eastern government implement a major budgeting reform across its ministries. I was part of the McBain team who worked on this sensitive project. My responsibility was to carry out the reform in one the largest ministries: the Ministry. As in most consulting projects, the schedule was tight and to make things more challenging, The Ministry was extremely resistant to change. In fact, prior to my involvement, several high level meetings had to take place to convince the Ministry to participate in the reform!

I experienced The Ministry's strong resistance on my first week of work. One of its key employees, a sixty-five year-old chief accountant named Ahmad was particularly against the reform – he had been compiling The Ministry's budget for thirty-seven years. During our first meeting, he categorically refused to share important documents I needed to start-off the project, and even screamed at me, claiming that I had a 'hidden agenda'. We had clearly started-off on the wrong foot! However, I quickly understood that Ahmad's support was vital to the reform's success. I decided to turn our relationship around.

To better understand the reasons of his resistance, I tried to organize a personal meeting with Ahmad. After several attempts, he accepted to meet at six in the morning – two hours before The Ministry opens its doors! I did not question his strange tactic or try to change the time of the appointment like others probably would have – instead I met his terms and showed up in The Ministry at six sharp. I still remember the shock on Ahmad's face when he saw me step into his office before sunrise. The meeting was the turning point for our relationship and for the project in general. It lasted for three hours, during which I let Ahmad do most of the talking and showed him how much I valued and respected his long experience. A feeling of mutual trust was quickly established, and Ahmad felt comfortable sharing with me his concerns. The underlying reason for his resistance was a fundamental lack of understanding of the reform. Unfortunately, the change was a top-down initiative and little communication was done to explain its features and advantages. As a result, everyone had his/her own interpretation.

After explaining to Ahmad the nature and benefits of the new budget processes, I suggested a set of initiatives to tackle his concerns regarding the lack of communication and transparency. To start off, I organized individual meetings with The Ministry's key staff, including the Minister and all department heads and invited Ahmad to attend. During these sessions, I took the time to explain the new processes and address any misinterpretation of the reform. In addition, I held daily jour fixes with Ahmad and his team to discuss the latest updates and come up together with solutions to the various problems that surfaced during implementation. These meetings were also an opportunity for me to train the accounting team on the new budgeting processes and give them the tools they needed to implement the reform in my absence. I was the only one from the McBain team to have taken such a personal and meticulous approach. And although it implied a longer working day than my team mates, I was very happy to see the results soon after. Indeed, these initiatives sustained Ahmad's trust in me and in McBain. They also transformed him from a serious opponent to the reform's biggest supporter. His endorsement was instrumental to the project's success: after only eight weeks and despite the initial resistance, The Ministry was one of the first ministries to fully implement the reform.

When Ahmad warmly embraced me at the end of the project, I couldn't help but remember our first meeting… and smile.

Navigating a Complex Financial Transaction

As a first year investment banking analyst, my managing director positioned me to lead the execution of a liability management transaction for an Ecuadorian bank. The task seemed daunting at first. I would need to work directly with the client to develop a revised financing plan. Then, I would oversee counsel to draft the plan into a prospectus. And finally, I would be responsible for presenting the plan to Latin American bond investors in order to win their consent. It was harrowing to realize that I would need to effectively navigate the needs and expectations of four different groups of professionals: counsel, investors, my boss, and ultimately the client.

The execution phase of a transaction is delicate, with several moving parts, different individuals involved, and counsels with various and often contrasting view points. Each aspect of the transaction must be negotiated among the parties of interest, and ultimately the transaction should (it is hoped) be completed to the satisfaction of the client.

When drafting the revised version of the prospectus for the transaction, the counsel struggled to accomplish the two most important tasks: (a) the new prospectus needed to correctly and legally satisfy the intentions of the Ecuadorian bank, and (b) the layout would need to be clear and concise so that bondholders could grasp and feel comfortable with the concept.

The counsel took a long time performing rounds of revisions, despite the client's needs to complete the transaction quickly. I confronted the head law partner about the timing dilemma, and he agreed to fewer rounds of revisions, but he also reminded me of the difficulties of restructuring the prospectus and the risks that were involved. It was better to take it slow and avoid mistakes. After consulting with my boss, I contacted the client, asking to push back the schedule to account for more rounds of editing.

Once the revised prospectus was completed, the hard part began: contacting the bondholders. Because the deal was relatively small, my boss entrusted me to perform the task usually completed by a member of our sales team. I needed to contact the Latin American bondholders personally, to explain the revised prospectus and receive their consent.

After calling multiple times and explaining the nature of the transaction, I still had difficulties convincing several bondholders. From their perspective, they had little motivation to cooperate. If I was to be successful, I would need to think creatively.

Because the non-consenting bondholders had relatively small positions, I proposed that we buy out any investors who refused to consent, despite possibly needing to pay above market price to do so. It would be worth overpaying for stray bond positions if it meant we could complete the main objective. My boss approved the idea, and I requested that our traders offer to purchase the non-consenting bondholder positions.

After several heated negotiation sessions with the bondholders, (some of whom only spoke Spanish), I finally derived the correct repurchase price. Our trading desk bought the small piece of bonds, and we were able to close the transaction – allowing the Ecuadorian bank to adjust its liabilities and importantly, for my bank to impress a client that had initially been skeptical about the success of the deal. The execution taught me that when managing different groups of professionals, persistence and, at times, creative problem solving is necessary.

Finding a Collegial Solution

By joining Colgate University TV, I discovered new ways of expressing myself creatively—editing video and creating television shows. My first production at CUTV was *Gate Update*, a weekly news show. At the beginning of senior year I collaborated with the Communications Office to use the state-of-the-art studio in the new library to stream our show on the Colgate website. However, my collaboration efforts put me in the middle of a serious conflict between Colgate's administration and the CUTV Executive Board. The Board thought that working closely with the administration would limit our independence. On the other hand, the administration fiercely opposed CUTV's idea to broadcast world news and weather segments, as those were deemed irrelevant for the Colgate website. The situation escalated into a string of angry emails sent back and forth, which threatened the continuation of the show.

I did not want to jeopardize my relationship with the Executive Board, of which I had been a part for four years. Nevertheless, I wanted this collaboration to work because I saw the obvious benefits—the HDTV equipment would greatly improve our broadcast's visual quality. Furthermore, our show would no longer be limited to the campus TV network—we could broadcast Colgate news to a much larger audience, promoting the school, and giving more exposure to those members of the crew who aspired to careers in television.

Hence, I decided to serve as mediator between CUTV's leadership and Colgate's administration. At first, I could not understand why my colleagues at CUTV so vehemently opposed collaboration with the administration. After lengthy discussions with the station's general manager, I began to understand his viewpoint: in essence, CUTV had invested a lot of time and effort into equipping its studio, and wanted to see it used. Additionally, they did not want to lose control over the content of the show.

Since I knew that we could reach a consensus, I met with the administrators to voice CUTV's concerns. I explained that even though I did not completely agree with the rest of the Executive Board, I understood their perspective and wanted to reach a compromise to ensure a successful collaboration. I suggested that we use the library studio to produce two versions of *Gate Update*—one short with content suited for the website, and one long with world news and weather. In addition, I asked that we use a larger CUTV logo, and highlight on air, in the credits, and on the website that *Gate Update* is a CUTV production. The administrators appreciated my honesty and proved willing to cooperate. At the next Board meeting, I proposed the agreement, explaining that the changes meant a more professional-looking show that could now reach students, parents, and alumni, thus becoming a marketing tool for the station. The Board voted to give it a try, and my efforts to improve the show succeeded.

What I learned from the experience was that life is not a zero-sum game, and that negotiations can appease group interests. My diplomatic efforts paid off, as Colgate eventually bought weather forecasting equipment for the studio and added that segment to the website version of the show. *Gate Update* continued after my graduation and can still be found on Colgate.edu. Moreover, the show facilitated the television careers of the crew—our anchor now works at ABC News and our weather girl was accepted to a graduate program in meteorology. While I am not pursuing a career in television, I hope to be able to apply my video editing and collaboration skills to the production of Wharton Follies 2012.

Lessons Learned from Working Across Business Units

After five months at Global White Goods Manufacturer, I was assigned the responsibility of backing up the marketing team of a particular brand. I had to structure the communication of the brand strategy, to support the Marketing VP in an important global meeting, held to review the investment focus by geographic region. From the beginning, I mainly interacted with the brand manager, who was responsible for the brand results. In a type of "business partner" role, I was first limited to following up on his team to ensure the quality of the deliverable within the 3- week deadline. However, within a period of two weeks, even after conversing with the manager, the material was still missing key strategy elements and I decided to take the lead on the task.

As I extended my participation, I discovered that since the brand launch two years before, little had been done in terms of strategy definition (e.g. consumer understanding, market sizing, competitive landscape study). I realized that, due to his background in sales, the manager was a very pragmatic, results-oriented person and did not believe that those strategy definitions would help his team achieve his sales objectives. The brand development had been mainly directed to achieve annual sales targets. For the following week, I worked closely with the manager to define macroeconomic strategy drivers and long-term goals for the business. I focused on explaining the quantitative and qualitative analysis necessary, hoping he would grasp the concepts.

We had clearly distinctive viewpoints, as he was mainly concerned about immediate action plans to ensure short-term sales results. On the contrary, I value a clear vision of the strategy to sustainably achieve long-term objectives and avoid risks and missed opportunities when concentrating only on short-term goals. Our different ways of thinking and distinct professional strengths made our interactions tense and taxing. It was challenging to convince someone in a higher position to see the importance of a well-grounded strategy and make him realize that he needed to fill gaps in strategy definitions for his business.

Despite the manager's discomfort in working on long-term plans, in a few days we developed a presentation that needed to be validated by the Marketing VP. Without solidly defined strategic drivers, it was a delicate situation to develop a superficial yet convincing presentation. As a result of the time restriction and little available information, I could see that there were still improvements to make on the material, but we agreed to stick to the deadline and present it to the VP. She asked me for refinements and suggested that I take a deeper dive into the existing business strategy. Trying to be diplomatic, I had a hard time explaining that the existing strategy was flawed while avoiding negatively commenting on the manager's performance. As a result, the VP took my recommendation to allocate resources to a project to review the business strategic drivers, since the brand manager was too consumed by the day-to-day operations.

Looking back, I realize that I could have the Strategic Planning director, about the lack of strategy in the business division ahead of time. She would have guided me regarding the approach with the brand manager and the communication of the situation to the Marketing VP, avoiding any inconveniences in my relationship with the brand manager. Finally, I could also have tried harder to work through the differences in reasoning between me and the manager, so that the work would be more efficient.

Managing Brazil-Swiss Agro Negotiations

When my fifth consecutive international case in McBain was presented to me, I did not realize it would become the most challenging one in my professional life. An agribusiness case with the McBain Zurich office offered me the chance to manage senior clients in Brazil, deal with different corporate interests in two countries, challenge a three-billion-dollar investment, and present the case findings to the most senior audience I had ever presented to. The case had been purchased in Zurich by one of the biggest commodity trading houses in the world, which wanted McBain's help to design a strategy for its new agribusiness in Brazil.

The first component of the challenge was the team structure. I was in Brazil with little support from a local McBain partner and with a client team composed of the local operations' president and leaders. In Zurich, the McBain team was composed of a partner, a principal and a consultant, and the client group included the board and a strategy leader. Although the Zurich team would come to Brazil some times and I would spend time in Zurich, I was the 24-year-old associate responsible for conducting the day-to-day relationship with the Brazilian client team.

Managing diverse interests between client teams was the second component of the challenge. While Zurich wanted to understand the business economics before developing a strategy, the Brazilian team wanted to structure some investment ideas and quickly have them approved by the board. As Zurich's position was more reasonable, I had to manage our local clients' expectations and have them contribute to something against their will. As a result, after complex argumentations and by showing them the importance of enhancing headquarters' knowledge about the current business, local clients started to cooperate in my task of building a business model.

The challenge was increased by a third component: the complex business model we built revealed a surprisingly poor economic performance for the investment and generated resistance in the local client team. Local traders refused the model's message by pushing for discussions about details and avoiding those about core issues. Those discussions happened in Brazil under my responsibility, although McBain in Zurich participated in some via calls. To succeed in this phase I had to take my modeling and negotiation skills to a next level. When discussing with local team's traders, I was benefited from having worked in a trading room during my internship at Banco Santander. I knew how traders' minds worked and could follow their reasoning, avoiding the pitfalls in their arguments.

In the end of this first phase of the case, I was asked to present the numbers to the client board and deliver the bad news. I was very anxious about presenting to an audience with double my age of experience in the industry, a task not so common to two-year associates. However, having calculated all the numbers and designed all the slides made me comfortable with the content of the presentation and guaranteed the meeting's success.

After the board's meeting and given the presented results, the McBain team focused on finding alternatives to improve the current investment's performance instead of analyzing additional investments. Although not expecting that outcome, both teams in Brazil and Zurich were satisfied to have addressed a problem that could have undermined their performance.

This was a challenging yet rewarding experience: we generated impact to the client by helping it understand and optimize its three-billion-dollar investment and I learned that my limits can always be pushed when I act with intelligence, courage and effort. I learned that despite my relative low seniority I can successfully lead tough client discussions, manage senior clients, resolve conflicts, and make presentations to a senior audience. My performance in this case earned me a promotion in McBain and encouraged me to keep looking for the most challenging opportunities in order to get the biggest apprenticeship and rewards.

Looking Out for a Friend and Learning a Valuable Life Lesson

When I arrived at the LSE, I came with the goals of bringing excellence both to the classroom and to campus life. I succeeded, bringing innovative thinking to class discussions and coursework. I also made my mark as a student leader, and my peers elected me to serve on the Executive Committees of the Development Society and of the Investment Society. However, in my second year of university I encountered a very challenging situation with my flatmate that put me in a difficult situation with my studies and my commitments to the societies I was involved with.

Thomas had been a very close friend of mine since boarding school and it was natural we became flatmates whilst at university. However, Thomas struggled to settle into life in London. His behaviour changed: he started frequenting people who exerted a bad influence on him, stopped attending classes, began sleeping during the day and staying awake at night, and he would often go missing without notice. As a close friend I became worried about him and suspected he might be suffering from depression. Concerned, I reached out to his brother, who also lived in London and who, given the family's traditional Indian background, had a lot of responsibility over him. When Thomas found out I had discussed the situation with his brother he was very angry, accusing me of conspiring behind his back. I felt guilty, and felt that I had somehow betrayed my close friend.

The situation came to a head when Thomas came home one night bloodied and bruised. He had clearly been involved in a fight. I confronted him and told him that I thought his behaviour was wrong, and that he was throwing his life away in London. At first he was angry, and refused to talk to me, but I insisted, telling him that he needed to get some help and sort out his troubles. I called his brother the next day and told him what had happened. Shocked, his brother decided to send him back home to Mumbai to be with his family and 'straighten up'.

I'll always view Thomas' departure with bittersweet emotions. On the one hand I lost a close friend. But on the other hand I am happy that I confronted him and told his brother what was happening, otherwise I fear Thomas' situation would have continued to worsen.

Whilst his departure gave me closure and removed a source of anguish from my life, it however put a lot of pressure on my financial situation. Honouring my rental obligations in the absence of Thomas' contributions was impossible, and I was forced to take on a part-time job as a claims assistant at ICHEIC to make up the difference. The time commitment of my job however meant that keeping up with my academics and honouring my student leadership positions became very difficult. By the time exams came around I was significantly behind the rest of my class. I worried a lot, fearful of not being able to get the results I had set out to achieve. But determined to salvage my academic experience, I formulated a plan, identified steps to achieve it, and worked diligently towards them. I delegated my duties in the societies, and during the holidays before exams I maintained the most rigorous study schedule I have ever put myself through. The hard work paid off: I earned four first class grades in all four classes, practically cementing my final first class grade a year early. More than the grade however, it was the journey that made it one of the most rewarding experiences and one of my greatest achievements. The ability to work under pressure and to prioritise and manage my time effectively are skills that have allowed me to continue achieving challenging targets in my career to date.

From McBain Consultant to a Change Initiator

As a second-year consultant at McBain, I assumed a significant leadership role on the buildup of risk quantification models and their implementation during an 'Enterprise Risk Management (ERM)' project for a leading Korean 'Engineering & Construction (E&C)' company. During the project, I learned to motivate and convince people to accept my idea by addressing their true concerns, providing practical benefits, and delegating adequate responsibilities.

The kick-off meeting with clients was mediocre at best. Clients showed no respect and raised doubts on the viability of quantifying risks in the E&C sector. Mr. Soon, a senior manager whose support was imperative for the successful quantification of risks, did not hide his hostility as he grunted "You have no idea how the E&C industry work. This isn't going to work."

At first, I thought it was due to my inexperience in risk management related projects and weak quantitative background. Thus, I prepared the workshop on risk quantification methodology – both in theory and in practice – to highlight the importance of ERM as well as my competence. While I was able to round up some enthusiasm from the clients, the majority remained uninspired and reluctant.

Frustrated, I approached the middle manager of the taskforce team with whom I developed a rapport over the past three months. He suggested that we contact each client individually in order to find out what was really bothering them.

Together, we conducted face-to-face conversations with clients and discovered a surprising fact: clients were uncooperative not because they viewed me as incompetent but because they feared that risk quantification would highlight their mistakes made in the past. It was then I realized that the intent of ERM was not clearly communicated throughout the client company.

To ease their fears, with the help of the McBain team management, I invited both the top management and working-level clients to a workshop. The client CEO clearly communicated that ERM was a tool for the future, not a tool to reprimand them. Then I showed how an implementation of the ERM could have potentially reduced mismanagement on past construction projects. Also, I emphasized that savvy risk management leads to architectural landmarks and symbols of prosperity while unscrupulous business decisions can cause public havoc such as the Asian financial crisis of '97. I reminded them that their decisions and actions can have huge ramifications on society.

I noticed immediate changes in the clients' behaviors. They were nodding their heads and some even took notes during my presentation. This could not be found during the kick-off meeting. Mr. Soon, a key senior manager, said "Now we are on the same page. Let's do this" as he patted my shoulder at the end of the meeting.

The meeting was a success. I persuaded and assigned four middle managers from different business units as the quality assurance officers of the risk quantification. I selected them on the basis of their knowledge of risks and their abilities as leaders and peer-motivators. We were prompt in our delivery of results, and to my surprise, our client teams quickly moved to quantify the risks for over 300 projects. Those who have actively participated in the risk quantification process became ardent supporters of ERM and began promoting the importance of ERM throughout the organization.

By seeking timely advice and attempting to sympathize and understand the clients' true concerns, I was able to win their trust, motivate them to give their best and lead them to achieve the collective goal. Driving change with new ideas can be exciting but it will not materialize without a united team. While I was able to motivate the clients by highlighting the practical benefits as a consultant, I learned that identifying and highlighting a common factor was the first step in uniting people.

Engagaing a New Analyst

My first opportunity supervising a new analyst, Bill, almost ended in failure due to my short-sighted behavior. With the combined productivity of two analysts on this deal, I assured my staffer that I would be able to still manage my other projects effectively. To maximize efficiency, I focused on the time-consuming financial modeling while delegating to John the peripheral tasks within an inexperienced analyst's capabilities. Although I had delivered on my deadlines, I was surprised when my staffer expressed his disappointment in my performance. Bill had complained to him that he felt disconnected from our project and had requested a reassignment.

I exacerbated this challenging experience by poorly communicating, both upwards and downwards. Eager to succeed in my first management role, I set unrealistic expectations for my staffer because I failed to factor in the time to properly train a new analyst. While my insistence on taking ownership proved invaluable in past projects, my inexperience in delegating responsibilities to others made me hesitant to relinquish control of the assignments, such as modeling, that were critical to the project's success. Focused on meeting my deadlines, I had not entrusted Bill with the modeling assignments that he desired. Inadvertently, my actions had alienated him from the project.

Despite spending many sleepless nights in the office, I realized that the demands of my other projects prevented me from devoting the adequate time to train Bill. I needed to invest more time upfront with him to provide the direction that he needed to complete the more challenging tasks. I communicated my time constraints to my staffer and received relief on my other projects. Going forward, I involved Bill in every step of the process. In dividing the deliverables our team expected, I gave him the lead in the modeling tasks per his request. Although the switch resulted in working even longer hours on our project, it allowed me to guide Bill through his mistakes and accelerated his development.

This experience taught me important lessons in communication and motivation. I should have been realistic about my time constraints with my staffer so that we could develop an effective plan of action. By taking Bill's input into consideration, he developed a greater sense of ownership for our project. Giving Bill the lead on some of the project's most important assignments kept him more engaged and led to better project outcomes. By changing my behavior, I forged a great working relationship and friendship with Bill.

I have continued to apply these lessons in communication and motivation in both my professional and extracurricular relationships. In discussions with my portfolio manager at my current role, I always am candid about my opinion, even when I disagree. This honesty has forged the trust that has been vital to our successful teamwork. While organizing fundraising events for academic programs supporting underprivileged children, I strive to create an environment that values the input of every member and gives each the responsibility to make important decisions. Rather than relying solely on my own abilities, I have learned the importance in cultivating a team culture among my colleagues. This collaborative approach has driven the success of our fundraisers and continues to attract new members to our non-profit organization. At Wharton, I plan on utilizing this approach to maximize my experience with my learning team and as a member of the Wharton community as a whole. The valuable lessons this challenging experience has taught me will continue to influence my leadership style in all aspects of my life.

Adapting Communication Styles to Manage Upwards

It was my third project at McBain and we were already two months in. In consulting, that's enough time to become a relative expert – in this case, global best practices in the modern retail channel for a fast-moving consumer goods company. I was responsible for designing a strategic shopper marketing program and implementation plan, something normally assigned to a senior analyst. I anticipated a challenge and carefully planned the framework, validating it with my manager and industry experts to ensure it was correct and realistic to accomplish in the timeframe.

It was at this time that a Summer Associate – an MBA intern – was assigned to work with me. A fellow American with an interest in Latin American business, Mark* and I quickly became friends. However, it soon became apparent that two issues would complicate our professional relationship. First, there was a natural dichotomy of interests – I was already an "expert" but Mark had no prior knowledge of the subject matter and he was expected to make a significant, independent contribution during his internship. Second, though Mark occupied a more senior position, he had never worked in consulting. Even though I only had 8 months of experience as an analyst, I was already adept at formulating and executing analyses and strategic frameworks under McBain's and our client's standards.

I invested a few days transferring my knowledge of shopper marketing to Mark, something that had taken me over a month to accumulate but that he needed to know immediately to meet our deadline in one month. During the following weeks, I checked in periodically, inquiring about progress while attempting not to undermine his seniority. He never approached me with questions, so I assumed he was executing his assignment. It soon came to my attention, however, that Mark had been trying to re-invent the framework instead of completing the current one. I couldn't seem to convince him that it was non-negotiable, and time was running out.

The timing went down to the wire. Mark and I had to work one weekend to complete a presentation by Monday morning. Sunday afternoon, Mark informed me that he did not know how to do his portion. At that point, I focused on the objective of completing the deliverable. In a desperate last attempt to salvage the presentation, I

---

* Name has been changed

drew very explicit outlines of the graphs, bullet points and structure. I explained how these pieces all fit together into the storyline and why they were critical elements of our recommendation.

All of a sudden, something clicked. Mark understood in an hour what I had assumed he knew all along. We began to work like a well-oiled machine and completed the presentation together by 3:00 AM. It went off without a hitch the next day, and Mark and I were proud of what we had accomplished.

This was the first experience in which I became fully aware of how critical it is to be attentive to other learning and communication styles. In my effort not to undermine his seniority, I had missed the cues that he needed more explicit guidance than I had given him. Once I drew the example, he immediately understood; evidence that he was a visual, not aural, learner. In discussing it with him later, Mark confirmed that attempting to make a new framework was how he grappled with trying to understand how the concepts flowed together. Since then, I have not only been more diligent in keeping track of the people on whom my workstream depends, but also have used varying communication styles before it becomes a compromising situation.

Subtle Techniques to Help a New Member of the Firm Integrate

'Ian, a first draft by the end of the week is just not going to happen! I've done this before and you need a detailed cash flow model which takes at least 3 weeks to build", this was going to be a long 4 months! I was running through weekly deliverables with the team, and as usual Tom was finding reasons to disagree.

It was the third week of a 4 month project. Besides myself, a Associate Consultant, the team consisted of a manager, two new Associate Consultants, and a new Senior Associate - Tom. Not only was Tom my senior, he had over 5 years banking experience compared to my 2 years at McBain. However, our manager still looked to me to lead the team and asked that I get Tom up to speed on McBain's consulting approach.

What had initially seemed a straightforward request that placed me in the familiar role of working with new hires, proved to be a real challenge. In planning discussions, Tom rattled off numerous reasons my approach would not work, but offered no constructive alternatives. He avoided questions about his work-stream and sat quietly in team content sessions, never offering any ideas of his own. Tom also kept distracting my manager with analysis tangential to our projects objectives in order to try and impress him outside of a team setting. Attempts to graciously make him aware that his behavior was counter- productive, Tom dismissed my comments and sullenly avoided me for the next few days. What frustrated me most about his attitude was that at work social events he seemed a very smart and motivated professional! I resisted involving my manager and instead I took a step back and saw room for improving my own approach. After all as Team Leader it was my responsibility to bring out the best in the whole team.

Though capable of developing content plans and moving the project-team forward on my own, I would ask Tom for his input. Although we still disagreed on setting priorities and the depth of analysis, the collaborative approach helped him perceive me as a partner rather than a rival. It also provided a convenient segue to discussing his work, allowing me to achieve the goal set by my manager, namely coaching him on the consulting mindset and approach at McBain.

I carefully applied this tactic to help Tom engage with the entire team. I would ask a junior associate consultant to practice explaining their analysis to Tom in advance of a client meeting. This ensured we used Tom's client relationship experience whilst also implicitly teaching him our core analytical methods. More importantly it helped identify his strength on the team and give him the confidence to contribute more actively in team discussions.

Finally in casual conversation I would suggest an analysis our manager might find useful that played to Tom's strengths, such as a summation of Wall Street views on competitors M&A deal. This helped focus Tom's efforts to build rapport with my manager and showcased his strengths on relevant issues.

Ultimately what enabled me to improve our working relationship was not the tactics I employed but being able to understand the situation from Tom's perspective. This mindset has proven invaluable in the foreign countries and organizations I have worked in, where it has helped me build trust and form healthy relationships with the people I meet and work with. This ability to empathize with team members or customers and develop solutions to address their needs is a skill I hope to hone going forward as it is the foundation of any future CEO.

4 A FAILURE AND LESSONS LEARNED

QUESTION

Describe a failure that you have experienced. What role did you play, and what did you learn about yourself? How did this experience help to create your definition of failure? (600 words)

INTRODUCTION

The failure essay is perceived by many to be the prototypical trick question. It is akin to when you are interviewing and someone asks for your weaknesses. You could answer, "I work too hard" or "I have a hard time delegating because I am a perfectionist." These are perhaps safe answers in an interview and the distant cousin to the failure essay. They are not, however, the same kettle of fish. Do not waste this essay being overly trite and missing the opportunity for more profound reflection and self-expression.

The essay must reflect not only a failure (of which we all have many when we are frank) but how you can use that failure to develop, grow, do things differently, and emerge as a changed person in some small but meaningful way.

The failures in this section demonstrate that mistakes, both small and large, can be windows into important personal and professional questions everyone faces at one time or another. The critical factor is reflecting on what happened and distilling down why it did not work. The logical next step is discussing how you successfully avoided it happening again.

If you are having trouble finding a good failure, fear not. This essay is an excellent time to think back on your work of the past few years and reflect on how you have changed and became a better manager, team player, or friend. Think about what subtle changes you have made and craft a story around that. It is an opportunity we rarely have time for so use it as a welcome respite. Just be sure to be clear and explicit about why it was a failure and why that failure mattered to you.

Learning From an Afghan School With No Students

The Noorzai school in Helmand Province was a typical victim of the Afghan war. The Taliban had torched the building when they discovered that girls were being educated there, and subsequent years of looting and vandalism had turned the ruined building into an opium den operated by corrupt local police. Over 400 children in the area had no school to attend, and the overall literacy rate in the area was approximately 5%.

As the civil affairs team leader, my mission in Afghanistan was to restore local institutions that had been affected by violence. The defunct school seemed an ideal candidate for renovation. The local children could continue their education and the community could begin to revive- I felt compelled to turn it around.

We sent in the military to evict the school's police squatters, who had been using the school as an illegal toll-collection site blocking the main road. Next, I brought in construction workers to replace the school's shattered walls, windows and doors. We spent thousands of dollars on everything from blackboards to soccer fields, and located several of the school's prior teachers, who agreed to return and instruct once the school re-opened. Finally we re-opened the school with an exciting celebration featuring a huge community feast and school supply giveaway, attended by over 200 village children.

Back at the base, I waited eagerly to hear that the students were flowing in. Nothing. Day after day, no children showed up for classes. None of the teachers were showing up either. The next week, as I walked alone through the empty school grounds, I wondered what had gone wrong.

Upon surveying some local families, I found out why the children were not attending school: parents were still concerned with the local security conditions for their children, and teachers were afraid to hold classes. When I asked them why- despite our aggressive security efforts- they felt concerned for their children's safety, one father said "Yes, things are safe for you- you have guns and wear armor. We are poor peasants- how can we protect our children at school when we are in our fields?"

My mistake was clear to me: I had been so in love with the idea of rescuing the school that I neglected to ask my Afghan 'customers' about the deeper issues facing their community. I should have first approached local elders and families to identify and deal with the underlying security issues before worrying about classroom paint colors, and balance my enthusiasm for the project with proper due diligence. While the Noorzai school was written off as a loss, I applied these lessons to another school renovation project the following month. This time, before we began building,

I surveyed local families about the security situation and worked out a protection arrangement with local police and the Afghan Army. With the critical community 'buy-in' that I had learned to secure, the second school's reopening was a success- every patrol that stopped by the school was greeted by hordes of rambunctious young schoolchildren eager to show us their latest penmanship strokes, and challenge us to pick-up soccer games.

In the military, I used to define failure as simply the opposite of mission accomplishment- a hill not occupied, a battle not won, or a school not in session. But through the experience I learned that the failure itself is not the ultimate defeat- victory was determined by what I did AFTER the failure. It made me realize failure can simply be part of the long-term strategy- so long as lessons are learned and applied to the next challenge.

From Beirut to Lebanon and Back

No eighteen-year old would want to fail on the very first important decision he takes as an adult. When I turned eighteen, I had a very critical choice to make: stay in Lebanon and enter the American University of Beirut (AUB) or travel to Paris and accept a full scholarship to one of France's most prestigious academic programs, 'Classes Préparatoires' at the Lycée Louis Le Grand (LLG). To give some context, 'Classes Préparatoires' consist of two years of very intensive and competitive education that prepares students for the entry exams of the country's leading business schools. The program was very selective: among the hundreds of Lebanese students who had applied, I was the only one admitted. And to make my choice easier, I was one of a handful of applicants to be granted a full scholarship from the French government.

Back then, I considered AUB as the traditional and straightforward choice. After all, most of my family members were AUB alumni. LLG, on the hand emerged as a more entrepreneurial and 'once in a lifetime' opportunity. In pursuit of new challenges, and against my parents' advice, I chose the Lycée Louis Le Grand.

However, three months after joining the program, I realized I had made the wrong choice. I was lured in by the challenge and prestige, and had, unfortunately, overlooked a very crucial factor, the curriculum. Even though, my performance was rather good, I had little interest in most classes and was overall disappointed with the program. However, I was too embarrassed to discuss it with my family and friends. After all, I had left the country against their advice. I was the one who turned down AUB hoping for more challenging opportunities. I couldn't just come back to Lebanon with my tail between my legs. Changing my opinion would have been admitting to be irresponsible. I was dreading the inevitable "I told you so" and I simply could not admit my mistake. After countless sleepless nights, I decided not to share my doubts and give the program another shot. The months that followed proved that I had completely lost interest in the 'Classes Préparatoires'. No matter what I did, I simply couldn't motivate myself anymore. What worried me most was that, I had lost my passion and couldn't therefore have fun or excel in my classes. At the end of my first year, my unhappiness affected my performance and my grades suffered.

My summer vacation turned into a sorely needed period of self-introspection. I realized then, that being responsible meant admitting one's mistake. I had failed in my decision and it was time to confront the truth. For the first time, I decided to share my feelings with my family. To my great surprise, I found them extremely understanding and supportive. Our discussion made me realize how immature it was for me to let pride cloud my judgment. I had failed twice: first by making a poorly-informed choice; and second, by placing my ego before facts. There was only one way to correct my mistakes, pull out from the 'Classes Préparatoires' and come back to Beirut.

Returning to Lebanon was no easy experience at all. It taught me that failure is always around the corner and is a natural component of any entrepreneur's route. However successful entrepreneurs recognize failure when they face it, they put their ego aside and ultimately correct their mistake.

A Lesson on Developing Human Resources

During one experience at McBain, I failed as a leader, neglecting to provide coaching to a subordinate. I worked as a coordinator, a module leader, on a three-month case for a family holding company that needed to evaluate its financial structure and improve profitability of one of the businesses. The project team was composed of a manager, a module leader and two analysts under my direct leadership. It was my responsibility to plan and allocate the tasks between them and follow the work evolution, managing the intermediate deliverables in accordance with the scheduled deadlines.

One of my subordinates was also my close personal friend and roommate. She was allocated to the case with the intention of developing her analytical skills and knowledge in finance. Keeping that in mind, I gave her the responsibility of developing the financial model in Excel. This tool was essential to base the conclusions and recommendations to the client. Her performance could determine her future in the company, with the risk of dismissal prospects if her results were below expected. As we were allocated to the client office out of São Paulo, the hotel routine and intensity of work made it difficult to talk as friends about her motivation for the job.

Accordingly, during the first weeks of the case, I was late in noticing that she was having a hard time performing some related activities, such as understanding specificities of the database and building analyses, to extract useful information and diagnose profitability opportunities.

Immersed in other work fronts and supporting the manager in the client relationship, I didn't provide my subordinate the coaching she needed in time. Consequently, we were off schedule in the beginning and the workload increased. With the deadline pressure, I decided to redistribute tasks among the three of us, instead of dedicating time to help her develop the required skills. At the end of the case, as her coordinator, I completed an honest evaluation of my friend's performance. She did not deliver what was expected from the beginning. I also pointed out my lack of coaching. Based on her previous case evaluations and this one, McBain's leadership decided to dismiss her, in a recessionary downsizing.

Although as a team we delivered all the expected recommendations to the client and received robust compliments, I failed to perform one of the most important responsibilities of a leader: developing human resources. To fail in the professional context while impacting a friend resulted in personal frustration and guilt.

Through this experience I define failure as the inability to achieve the objectives of all people involved in a task, either as a group or individually. Hence, even when tangible results are successfully achieved, failure may be the outcome if one of the involved people is disappointed with his participation.

I learned that motivation is fundamental to self-satisfaction and outperformance. Thus, it is indispensable to ensure a healthy work environment, respecting people's limits when setting goals. Most importantly, I learned that dedicating time to coaching and developing people is a main factor of success in any job. Since then, I've been applying these lessons in my leadership style. For instance, at Whirlpool, the director of the water division asked for my support to coordinate a trainee in a new business opportunity project. Besides providing her guidelines to build a work plan, define analysis and develop a business case, I took the opportunity to talk about her career alternatives in the company and to coach communication skills and upward expectations management. Later on, the director thanked me for contributing to her development and praised my work style among other directors.

Learning to Seek Opportunity in a Challenging Relationship

Being hired as a derivatives trader right after graduating from Law School was, above all, a daily challenge. For the first months, every day I would ask myself "Can I do this? Can I be a trader?" But after a while, the question changed to "How can I become an excellent trader?"

By then, I had proved to myself that I had the quantitative and analytical abilities and communication skills. Observing my colleagues, I realized I did not want to be just another trader. I wanted to be like them, impressively talented professionals, with ideas to improve our business, the relationship with clients, operational systems and revenues. I was part of a small team from which I learned new things every day, both personally and professionally.

After two years as a trader and no longer with questions haunting me, BankBoston Brazil was acquired by Itau. The bank was on its way to expand operations and client base. New traders were hired and the team more than doubled. The person assigned to be my supervisor was one of the newly hired professionals, but he had no previous experience in derivatives sales. After working so closely to those I considered the best in the market, it was frustrating to have the strategy of the team outlined by someone who did not possess the expected technical knowledge nor was interested in the development of those below him.

I started to feel uninspired. My search for excellence was not valued and he provided me with no coaching at all. After some months, we were working independently and did not share experiences or knowledge. I felt my personal and professional growth compromised by not having a leader-like boss and I became more and more individualistic. And because of my frustration and impatience, I failed to assess his capabilities, for example, his undeniable talent in building professional networks. So I have reflected a lot about the 1-year period we've worked together (eventually he was laid off as he was considered unfit) and I feel that I could have worked with him in a more constructive manner. I neglected that even if he was not a role model, I could still learn from him.

As history repeats itself, two years ago when I was already working as a Fixed Income Associate, a new team was incorporated to our unit. One of the hired VPs had worked for years in NY and was an expert in international fixed income, but had no experience in the Brazilian market. Having learned from my mistakes, I saw it as an opportunity to work as a team and develop myself. I realized that this attitude could leverage both his and my work. I helped him with my knowledge of the local market and consequently our team was assigned important transactions. As our professional relationship was based on trust and mutual learning, he had always been extremely helpful and enjoyed coaching me. Each one had weaknesses, but as a team we were great. Moreover, I'm sure this cooperation model created positive feelings amongst other team members. As a consequence, even being an associate, I am now considered a reference for mid-sized companies' local fixed income transactions in Itau, since I gained the team's confidence to lead such deals.

For me, failure is not making the best possible use of the available resources and not reaching the best possible outcome. I still believe that a powerful feature of leadership is the ability to inspire others. But I've learned from my failure that working as a team is just as important in order to deliver great results and to create a good working environment. I realize now that every person that crosses our professional path has something to teach us. It is our duty to remain humble and open even when the situation appears to be negative.

Mastering Inclusion to Motivate a Diverse Group

In my second year at Atlantic College, I was keen to make an original contribution to such a dynamic setting and so co-founded the Environmental Action Society. Seeking to start strongly, the co-founder Yassir and I organized a school-wide conference on renewable energy, recruiting a leadership team and contacting impressive speakers, including the shadow energy minister of the Welsh assembly and the head of Oxfam in Wales. Unfortunately, two out of three guest speakers never showed and conference attendance was poor. Yassir and I retreated to draw our lessons-learned.

We determined the primary reason for the event's failure was that we had not utilized our leadership team to its full potential. We had taken on most of the work ourselves, leaving other members with little to do and little enthusiasm. If we had delegated key tasks to specific leadership team members, such as following up with speakers, the event could have been much more successful and enthusiasm for the event would have spread more widely.

Eager to rectify the situation, I convened a meeting and led our leadership team to brainstorm ways of improving the society and to lay the foundations for its success. We assessed how we could have made the conference better. I also set forth a strong vision for the group, and, having gained consensus for the vision, we altogether identified steps to achieve it. By delegating tasks to members based upon their strengths and passions, I also managed to re-ignite enthusiasm amongst the team.

This proved to be an important turning point. For the rest of the year, our leadership team was united and moving toward our designated goals. With a strong marketing plan, we communicated the relevance of our group to the student body. Enthusiastic, our members did an outstanding job at organizing lectures and talks, and stimulating debate amongst students about environmental issues. At the year's end, the Environmental Society was awarded 'Best New Society of the Year' and received a £2,000 prize for "outstanding contributions" to the student community.

Despite the disappointment of the failed event, the experience was an important lesson. It sharpened my leadership skills and made me adept at harnessing the talents of team members, which has helped me achieve excellence both throughout my professional career and in my current community service roles. For instance, as a volunteer on the Great Britain United World College National Committee I formed part of the team that organised the Fun Run, a charity event aimed at raising funds for a scholarship that enabled a student to attend the Waterford Kamhlaba United World College of Southern Africa in Swaziland. I knew from past experience how important it was for everyone to have designated tasks and responsibilities so as to ensure their motivation and commitment, particularly when this was on a volunteer/part-time basis outside of normal work commitments. By ensuring everyone had designated tasks, the team worked extremely well together and ensured the success of the final event.

The experience also taught me that failure is often a useful contributor to ultimate success, no matter what the endeavour. Failure can be the most important way to learn from one's mistakes and to find a way of improving a situation for the better. I therefore learned not to be afraid of failure, and that trying and failing is better than not trying at all. So despite my inability to secure a summer internship position in investment banking in the summer of my second year at university, I gathered the lessons-learned from that experience and used them mount an even better search for a full-time position the following year, ultimately successfully securing my employment at Morgan. The belief that trying and failing is better than not trying at all is something which has helped me throughout my career and proved an invaluable lesson.

Learning Strategic Negotiations and the Importance of Being Assertive

As soon as I hung up the phone, a sinking feeling came over me. My mind raced to determine if I should go back on my word or risk losing over a thousand dollars – money I couldn't afford to lose. Not wanting to admit that I made a mistake and call back my Mexican landlady to tell her I would not be paying the last month's rent for fear that she would not return my security deposit, I just prayed that I would see the money again in 60 days as she promised. My roommate had already left the country and put me in charge of recovering our shared deposit, and the last thing I wanted to do was let her down.

Just as expected, the landlady called on the 20th of the month before my final rent payment was due, asking me to pay ahead of time because she was short on cash, again. I had rehearsed how I would tell her that we would not be paying the rent in lieu of her returning our security deposit. She didn't miss a beat, retorting that we were contractually obligated to pay the rent and she would return the deposit only after ensuring that no damage had been done. Perhaps because I naively believed that there would be severe repercussions if I didn't oblige, or perhaps because I wanted to believe this frail old lady was incapable of taking advantage of me, I suddenly heard myself agreeing. I didn't even try to negotiate.

After many months of repetitive calls and visits to the landlady, I was only able to recover a few hundred dollars. What should have been a straightforward transaction turned into a drawn out nightmare. Even though the consequences were minimal, the situation affected me very deeply. If I couldn't be assertive facing a feeble old landlady, how would I possibly survive in a cutthroat business negotiation? It evolved into a self-reflection on my values and an acknowledgment that I still lacked some basic awareness of strategic tactics if I wanted to be a successful negotiator.

I define this as a failure for three main reasons: I was most bothered by the fact that I didn't listen to my instinct, letting myself be bullied by empty threats from a powerless landlady. Then, I missed an opportunity to rectify the situation by simply not making the deposit while I still had the chance. Lastly, I realized that my relationship with the landlady was not nearly as important to me as the one I had with my roommate and friend, and I was ashamed at having mixed up my priorities. With targeted issues to work on, I resolved to never let this happen again, especially during an important situation with more at stake.

I have already applied more assertiveness in defending things important to me, particularly in negotiating a 6-month transfer to McBain's San Francisco office, in order to receive a benefit that I had clearly earned but was being asked to forego. Similarly, I rehearsed my negotiation strategy before discussing the issue with the Human Resources Director, but this time I was confidently ready with a counter offer and a well thought out justification of why I deserved to receive a transfer assignment. I am proud that I was able to apply the lessons I learned from a seemingly irrelevant issue to obtain a business opportunity that was important to me.

Mastering Soft Skills in the Netherlands

The completely bilingual team of project managers and engineers continued speaking Dutch as I entered the room. It was my first major meeting with a flagship client. We had been brought in to devise the strategy for a semiconductor manufacturer but our analyses concluded that the company was hemorrhaging cash. We had to act fast to avert bankruptcy. I was new to consulting, the only American, and not an expert in technology. I threw myself into the task with an unwavering determination to prove myself and deliver results for the president and company.

I tried to drive the process with maximum professionalism but was blind-sided during the presentation. My analysis on an important piece of market share data was wrong. I had pushed hard for a junior member at the client to give me information and subsequently found out that he had perceived me as rude and overly "American" in our interactions. He had given me information but omitted to mention that merger plans would impact the market's composition. While presenting to a senior vice president, the client team outright contradicted the validity of my analysis. I could almost see the steam coming out of the vice president's ears as he saw an expensive consultant destroying value.

I realized that the Dutch were friendly but private people, for whom relationships were important, and took this into consideration. I had neglected a strength from my personal life: forming relationships with people of varying cultures and backgrounds. What I had perceived as professional and hard-driving was perceived as "American" and insensitive.

I began socializing informally and empathizing with what was a challenging time. The company had laid off 1,000 people and was driven by demanding private equity owners. I learned some Dutch phrases and connected with the team over fried egg lunches and Heineken beer. I learned they were terrified of losing their jobs. Over the course of our relationship, proactive engagement and teamwork flowed naturally.

Against a backdrop of trust and friendship, the team accepted that I was focused on growth and not job cutting. They invited me to events outside of the office and trusted me to coach them on Excel and communicating technical concepts to private equity owners. The more I was myself and showed that I understood their culture and situation, the more impact I had. I was requested to stay longer and developed relationships that I maintain today. The work was successful and the company went public in 2010.

I learned that in order to succeed, I have to pay close to attention to balancing a drive for results with interpersonal connection. I have learned that skills in my personal life can be used to great effect in business, which does not operate in a vacuum. On a project I was on in Warsaw, I set aside time with Polish analysts I was coaching to share personal stories and understand their working styles. They introduced me to pierogi dinners and I adjusted to frequent coffee breaks that kept morale high. The lesson of personal connectedness and empathy has been invaluable in my work with clients and teams across multiple countries.

Failure to me is not an accident or act of carelessness, but something caused by a lack of self-awareness. Charging ahead without adequate attention to my clients and their situation was something I could have avoided by using skills from my personal life. A failure, however, is also a terrific opportunity to learn. I have countless times used the power of personal connection and empathy to build strong relationships, which has greatly increased my effectiveness.

Selling Acrobatics in Japan

In 2006, I almost went out of business due to my over-optimism as a new entrepreneur. I fell from financial solvency to US$20,000 in debt and escaped the situation only after humbly recognizing the Japanese market's expressed enthusiasm for my work as polite lip-service. To this day, I still apply the international business insights and personal lessons I learned from this experience.

Working at the Aichi Expo, I befriended managers from leading Japanese advertising/entertainment companies. They paid me interest and respect as a half-Japanese MIT graduate working in the entertainment business. I suggested to them that with my network of circus contacts and with Cirque du Soleil (CDS) about to open a permanent show in Tokyo, we could market competitive CDS-style entertainment to their clients. They supported my idea.

Without a concrete example of such work, however, the same story was to play out over and over: my friends would set up a meeting for me with a great contact; I would present my case in a 40th floor Tokyo meeting room; I would be told that my proposal was "very interesting"; and on the way out, I would be told about a new contact that "I really should meet." It was a flattering cycle, and unfortunately, I was too impressed with my own selling ability to realize that I was running in place, spending resources, and getting nowhere.

I had fallen prey to a classic blunder: just because a client expresses interest and enthusiasm doesn't mean that they are willing or able to offer concrete support. I was just being given a very enthusiastic and polite run-around. Worse, I was totally aware that this pitfall existed before I fell for it myself – I had just never considered that it could happen to me. What a lesson in humility.

Luckily, a project in Taiwan temporarily relocated me and helped me to see the situation from the perspective of a manager of a large project. I returned to Japan a year later with the successful Taiwanese project as an example of my proposed content, complete with production models, marketing strategies, and audience data. Instead of moving back to Japan, I would spend only a week at a time between projects on a sort of "victory lap." The strategy worked. I gave the appearance of a busy and successful international producer whose star was on the rise – "Act now or risk missing the boat!"

Soon thereafter a prominent member of the Japanese entertainment industry called me to source acrobatic content and to act as acrobatic coordinator for a major production. It was the first of several major New Circus Asia projects in Japan.

I learned a great deal of humility from my experiences trying to sell nonexistent things to people who didn't know they needed them. I learned that, without candid self-evaluation, I was just hitting my head against very well-padded, sympathetic walls. Most importantly, however, I also learned that there are creative solutions to even the bleakest problems.

PROPOSE A CLASS THAT WHARTON COULD INCLUDE IN ITS NEW CURRICULUM

QUESTION

Student and alumni engagement has at times led to the creation of innovative classes. For example, through extraordinary efforts, a small group of current students partnered with faculty to create a timely course entitled, Disaster Response: Haiti and Beyond, empowering students to leverage the talented Wharton community to improve the lives of the Haiti earthquake victims. Similarly, Wharton students and alumni helped to create, Innovation and Indian Healthcare Industry, a course which took students to India where they studied the full range of healthcare issues. If you were able to create a Wharton course on any topic, what would it be? (700 words)

INTRODUCTION

This was an experimental essay for the Wharton application. It sheds some light on the kind of innovative, progressive and student-led activity common at the school. Students take a leadership role unparalleled at any other top business school and student initiatives and suggestions around possible new courses are taken very seriously.

This essay also brings up an excellent opportunity to be both thoughtful about one's own experience and contribution, but also more technical and prescriptive. It is an excellent opportunity to shed light on the kind of contributions you might make in the classroom, based on your unique professional, geographical, and life experiences. Wharton prides itself on being a rigorous and analytical program and this essay demonstrates the kind of specific content that Wharton likes to develop, a mixture of the case and lecture style.

The Economics of Blood Distribution

Given the shortages at many community blood centers that resulted from the late-December snowstorms along the Eastern seaboard, it is confounding that there is no consensus among academics, blood donation professionals and hospital administrators regarding the most effective methods to increase blood donation. I propose the following course to delve further into this issue.

Course Syllabus: The Economics of Blood Donation

I. Overview

Approximately 15 million units of blood are needed annually in the United States for blood transfusions, many of which are life-saving, yet only three percent of the population donates blood. The objective of this course is to consider various approaches to incentivizing blood donation from both a conceptual and a practical framework. Students will compare Richard Titmuss's seminal work in the analysis of prosocial behavior, *The Gift Relationship*, in which he concludes that financial self-interest crowds out altruism, to the results of a selection of empirical studies that have been conducted in various countries during the last five years. Divided into groups, students will conduct a hands-on examination of how incentives effect blood donation by hosting blood drives using incentives they devise.

II. Course Materials

Required Text: Titmuss, *The Gift Relationship: From Human Blood to Social Policy* (1971)

webCafé: Materials for the project, selected readings and exam material will be posted for student access on webCafé. Readings may include but will not be limited to:

- Pererira, The Economics of Blood Transfusion in the 21st Century (2007)
- Mellstrom and Johannsson, Crowding Out in Blood Donation: Was Titmuss Right? (2008)
- Goette and Stutzer, Blood Donations and Incentives: Evidence from a Field Experiment (2008)
- Abolghasemi, Hosseini-Divkalayi and Seighali, Blood Donor Incentives: A Step Forward or Backward (2010)
- Wildman and Hollingsworth, Blood Donation and the Nature of Altruism (2009)

III. Prerequisites and Course Registration

This course is available to second year MBA students as an elective in the fall 2012 semester. Due to its limited size (15 students), only students registered for the course will be permitted to attend class following the auction.

IV. Class Format and Grading

In-Class Participation (10%): Students are expected to attend class and be prepared to discuss the weekly assigned reading. I will lead classes in which voluntary participation is expected by everyone.

Group Project (50%): Students will form three groups of five before the third class. Each group will be responsible for strategizing an incentive-based scheme that maximizes blood donation, as well as promoting and implementing a one-day blood drive, in collaboration with the American Red Cross Blood Services, Penn-Jersey Region, that utilizes that scheme. Each blood drive must occur at a different location on the university campus excluding Steinberg-Dietrich Hall, Huntsman Hall and other areas generally understood as comprising the Wharton campus. As blood donation is in shortest supply in the colder months, each blood drive must take place on Wednesday, November 14. Each group must prepare a PowerPoint presentation outlining their approach and analyzing their successes and failures. Each group will have 45 minutes to deliver its presentation at a special meeting of the class to occur on December 4. While the number of units donated may be a factor in a group's grade to the extent it indicates that a group's commitment to the project was above or below expectations, the groups will be graded primarily on their approach to the project and their presentation.

Individual Essay (40%): In lieu of a final exam, students will be required to complete a 4000 word final essay by 5 p.m. December 21 in which they state a case for what they conclude to be the best approach to incentivizing blood donation based on the assigned reading, any additional research they wish to conduct and the results of the group projects. Students are not required to support the approach they took in the group project and will not be penalized for advocating for all or part of another team's approach.

Greening Global Organizations

Consider this prospective case study: a multibillion dollar corporation with over 507 facilities around the world- four times the building real estate of Wal-Mart- and operating a fleet of over 160,000 vehicles is looking to reduce its yearly energy costs, currently estimated at $20 billion. Would Wharton students want to learn more?

The course, "From Swords to Sustainable Energy- 'Greening' the US Military" - would be a case study for how global organizations might implement energy conservation technologies to improve their profits and reduce fossil fuel dependence. For the Department of Defense, reducing reliance on fossil fuels impacts more than the bottom line: approximately 50% of all military convoys involve fuel transport, and for every 24 convoys sent out in war zones, one service-member is killed. In Afghanistan, the delivery cost of a single gallon of fuel can reach over $400, once security and logistics expenses are included. The Secretary of the Navy recently mandated that his service must cut its use of fossil-fuel derived energy in half by 2020.

The course would cover the military's energy demands from a business and logistical standpoint, the technological challenges and opportunities facing the Defense Department, and the strategic management challenges faced by such a large organization in implementing these solutions. I believe many student groups within Wharton would be interested in this class. Entrepreneurial Management majors interested in emerging alternative energy markets or securing startup funding might look to the Defense Department as a first customer. Wharton students with engineering backgrounds seeking to find out more about technologies sought by the Defense Department, where their areas of expertise might be applied, would also benefit. Students in the Business and Public Policy major would gain insight into how government and business organizations can form partnerships to improve resource sustainability. Environmental and Risk Management majors will contribute to class dialogue involving the military's impact on the environment and pollution. Strategic and Multinational Management students will become familiar with the challenges of coordinating alternative energy policies in an organization that spans six divisions and two million employees spread across the globe.

I can think of no better person to teach my proposed course than Stanley Laskowski, a professor who is already teaching courses at Wharton on Innovative Environmental Strategies. Drawing on his experiences as a senior government leader and a scientific expert, Professor Laskowski can bring an interdisciplinary approach that bridges the business, technical, and public issues and engage Wharton students into coming up with creative and collaborative ways to both increase our national security and improve the economy. In addition, the course would continue the Wharton tradition of supporting diverse teaching methods by using a variety of outside sources. Senior military leaders such as Admiral Mike Mullin have recently come to Wharton to speak about leadership issues, and would no doubt return to share their vision of the armed forces' energy independence with America's future business leaders, who can help execute that vision.

A unique component of the course would be 'Energy Treks.' I envision co-sponsoring trips to military bases in conjunction with members of the Wharton Energy Club, to get a first-hand look at the alternative energy efforts the US military is field testing. Having attended a Wharton Energy Club meeting during my school visit, I know there is tremendous interest in Wharton students to learn about emerging opportunities in the energy field. An example of such an Energy Trek would be a trip to Quantico, Virginia, where the Marine Corps is testing an Experimental Forward Operating Base which mimics the energy requirements of an expeditionary base in Afghanistan or Iraq. Its solar-powered water purifiers provide hundreds of gallons of potable water each day, and hybrid wind/solar generators cut diesel generators' fuel consumption in half. Wharton students would use their creativity to find applications for such technologies outside the military- providing off-grid solar power to remote African villages, or clean water in disaster-ravaged Haiti.

By harnessing the power of Wharton's diverse and innovative student body, the course will tap into the creativity of my colleagues and future alumni as we increase the national and economic security of our nation, and reduce the carbon footprint of other organizations and communities around the world.

Media in Emerging Markets

Entertaining the Next Billion Consumers:
Media & Entertainment in Emerging Markets

In Mumbai, you simply can't miss the 100,000 three-wheeled auto-rickshaws, fitted with neon lights, speaker systems and images of Hindu Gods and Bollywood actresses. On a humid night in Mumbai, I requested music. The driver plugged a USB thumb-drive into his stereo system. I then learned that he refreshed with the latest Bollywood songs for one rupee each at a local Internet café. It immediately struck me that this, like Unilever's one rupee shampoo packets, was the face of the future of the M&E industry.

I'd be thrilled to work with Wharton faculty, such as Professors Jehoshua Eliashberg and Peter Fader, the M&E club, the WIMI, and fellow students to develop a course that would prepare students for opportunities like the "one rupee song," inherent in M&E in emerging markets. The course would share concepts with some of Wharton's cutting-edge international offerings: *Multinational Management, Inside Indian Business, Business in the Global Political Environment, and Monetizing Emerging Interactive Media.* I envision a course essential not just for those interested in M&E, but for all Wharton students who will chase growth in emerging markets from the next billion consumers.

I would bid aggressively for this elective because of its timing and relevance. Global M&E is evolving fast, leaving much to learn. Digitization, the Internet, global expansion, and unprecedented exposure and consumer expectations in emerging markets have coincided with stagnating domestic markets. Giants like Sony and Disney have rushed to emerging economies to find that they required a radically different approach. Future success will belong to leaders who can move quickly, think locally, and adapt ingeniously.

I would bring my experience creating content for South Asian markets in traditional M&E channels, as a production manager with WAK Media, and an actor living and working in India. I have a strong understanding of the business models and trends in the conventional film, music, and television industries. I have keen awareness of the specific local challenges, industry structures, and major competitors in the South Asian M&E space. I've learned the importance of localizing content firsthand while developing television content for MTV Pakistan and doing voiceover work for Sony Television in India.

I hope to learn about new/digital media, and other emerging markets such as Brazil, Russia, and China from Wharton faculty and fellow students. A perfect research and development partner for the disruptive-technology/digital-media component of the course is the WIMI. WIMI faculty, and students from technology and digital-media backgrounds, would explore the effects of mobile, search, social networks, and video-on-demand in emerging markets. Students and faculty with experience in other high-growth countries can share knowledge of the local nuances that will change the way M&E companies do business there. The questions I have are endless: In the light-speed migration to platforms like Twitter and Facebook, what will become of traditional media? More Indians have cell phones than have access to toilets – what does 3G/4G technology mean for the global potential of mobile media? With rampant Internet piracy and free content, where will the revenue come from?

The course would be conducted in a discussion format, based on cases, readings, and media clips and interactive exercises to viscerally experience the media discussed and keep students engaged. Topics would include technology, distribution, regulation, local competition, localizing content, leveraging local talent, marketing, pricing, and piracy. The course would also dedicate time to debating the social power and accompanying responsibility of M&E in a largely illiterate and developing country like India, where film stars are literally considered gods and film possesses unparalleled power. The final team project would be to design a region-specific entry strategy for a division of an established Western M&E company – for example CNBC in Brazil, or Warner Brothers in China – addressing short and long term strategies relating to revenue models, pricing, sales, marketing, regulation, JVs and partnerships, competitors, metrics, and risks.

In addition to the curriculum, I would be happy to work with my contacts in India and the M&E club to bring in guest speakers such as India's leading film producer, Yash Chopra, or UTV's Ronnie Screwvala, who revolutionized the TV industry and brought Disney to India. With Wharton's reputation in India, this is absolutely feasible: Bollywood star Abhishek Bachchan came to the *Wharton India Economic Forum* a year ago to speak about many of the topics this course would cover.

Ethics of Profitability in Latin American Microfinance Institutions

The concept of microfinance began in the 1970's, with an attempt to demonstrate that poverty stricken women could be relied upon to repay small microcredit loans if given the opportunity. The founder of microfinance, Nobel Prize winner Mohammed Yunus, hoped to extend realistic financing options to the poor, without the exorbitant money lending rates that larger and more profitable institutions offered. At the time, his dream for the impoverished in Bangladesh seemed lofty, but by refining and creating an accepted cultural practice surrounding microcredit, he sparked an industry that has grown over 30% annually.

As the industry begins to mature beyond its infancy, it has begun to achieve what many academics and philanthropists had hoped it would eventually produce: profitability. This profitability has triggered interest from the same large institutions that had initially shunned the concept of microfinance, namely large financial firms. These institutions had previously only been willing to serve wealthier clients, with larger deals and juicier fees. However, in a display of the evolving microfinance environment, SKS Microfinance, an Indian institution founded by CEO Vikram Akula, recently issued an IPO for approximately $350 million that was oversubscribed by 13.5x. The popularity of this issuance clearly demonstrates that investors hope to profit from microfinance operations.

The SKS IPO and others like it have sparked an ethics debate in the microfinance community, primarily because of a fear that shareholder interests will be placed before the interests of the poor. Mohammed Yunus (2010) has publicly stated the following:

"By offering an IPO, you are sending a message to the people buying the IPO there is an exciting chance of making money out of poor people. This is an idea that is repulsive to me. Microfinance is in the direction of helping the poor retain their money rather than redirecting it in the direction of rich people."

This class will explore both sides of the argument from the perspective of Latin American microfinance institutions (MFIs), which are at the forefront of the profitability debate since they are some of the most profitable MFIs. To some champions of microfinance, the word "profitability" has become a dirty word. However, profitability is likely to be the key to microfinance sustainability – forcing microlenders to cover their costs, allowing them to obtain financing and technical expertise needed for expansion, and keeping them focused on providing efficient services to their customers.

How much profitability is necessary and/or ethical to sustain microfinance operations? In Latin America, there is a wide variation in the level of profitability registered by the various types of MFIs, with some maintaining very high levels and others performing less well. Finamerica in Colombia, for example, is forced to operate with a government-imposed interest rate ceiling that makes it extremely hard to break even. On the other end of the spectrum, Compartamos in Mexico and ProCredit in Nicaragua display very high returns.

Prerequisite classes would likely be in accounting and financial statement analysis. The class would evaluate in detail, the financial profile of prevalent Latin American MFIs. For example, an interesting topic could explore the ROE level needed among institutions in Latin America to support operations. Currently, ROE in Latin America has remained high, in the low 20 percent range. In some cases, such as Compartamos, it has been more than twice that range because of the high level of interest rates charged. Relatively high profitability is required to provide the retained earnings to support the capital base needed for a rapidly growing institution.

The class will explore the drivers of profitability among MFIs, including the maintenance of high loan portfolio quality, market interest rates, transaction costs, and efficiency in the face of growing margin pressure on interest rates.

A class that explores these topics would be a fantastic experience for me, since I have been active in Latin American microfinance organizations over the past few years. I am currently in beginning stages of creating a 501(c)(3) organization to benefit Latin American microcredit, with the hope of registering it and recruiting volunteers for the NYC Marathon in 2011.

Serving the Aged in Emerging Markets

I would create a course called "Constructing Services for an Aging Population in Emerging Countries." It would prepare executives and entrepreneurs interested in contributing to the quality of life of the elderly with business ideas, initiatives and experiences from various backgrounds and cultures.

To do this, the course would start with classes focused on the demographic and macroeconomic situation of countries in Latin America and Asia, whose promising economies present higher and more stable growth rates. Analysis of historical data and projections of the age pyramid of each country would be accompanied by descriptions of societal roles by age range, focusing on the growing percentage of the elderly.

Regarding the private sector, the professor would present an assessment of currently available services in selected countries for low, middle and high income elderly, identifying areas of improvement and new opportunities in each country for now and the following decades. He or she would also present successful companies and their innovations both within emerging economies and in developed countries, identifying benchmarks. The assessment would include studies on the most demanding service areas, including healthcare, entertainment, finance and transportation, all of which require customized solutions to senior citizens.

For example, a detailed evaluation of the conditions of healthcare services in Brazil would analyze service quality and availability, both regional and economic, of nursing homes, clinics, laboratories and hospitals throughout the country. With my special interest in this area due to my family's experience with its geriatric clinic, I could contribute to class discussions with examples of market demands for healthcare services. I could also invite professionals and academics within the network of my father, a geriatric physician, to speak regarding their experiences and difficulties developing the sector.

Students would have classes on senior citizen financial and entertainment services for different social segments. One of the class assignments would require that students brainstorm and propose solutions for entertainment services, such as artistic and cultural courses, exhibitions, touristic trips, customized hotels and others. The solutions should have the mission of making these services a part of senior citizens' daily activities in all socioeconomic levels, improving affordability and availability.

Another topic of the course would concern the role and presence of each country's government in the sector. Students would, learn for instance, that in Brazil, public hospitals and clinics are rare, underdeveloped and overpopulated. Existing financial assistance is limited and works as a palliative tool only. As the government does not have enough resources to invest in improving senior citizens' quality of life, it has an essential obligation to incent and even fund the private initiative to develop the sector. Future incentive model scenarios would be presented, based on different existing models around the world, including developed economies, as a way to help build the non-profit strategy for developing the sector.

As a major deliverable and the experiential learning portion of the course, students would work in groups, following the model of the Field Application Project program. They would select a case within a defined service sector and emerging country either to recommend an innovative solution for a developmental barrier of an existing company or to fulfill a major gap in service availability through non-profit systems. Students would have to detail the business plan, specifying operational and financial structure.

In order to have a clearer notion of the sector dynamics in the selected country, each group could seek funding from local companies to travel to visit the main cities and regions. During the trip, students would visit these companies, talk to their executives and get closer to local culture and traditions, helping them better understand the main drivers that should be worked on to get to an applicable and viable recommendation. After evaluation, the results of each group could be sent to host companies and non-profit institutions asking for support to overcome a barrier or find ways to grow the business.

With the help of Wharton's clubs, such as Wharton Asia Club and WHALASA, and faculty (especially regarding healthcare and social development, such as Patricia Danzon and Carol McLaughlin), the course could provide students with the knowledge and practical reference they need to have a professional experience within the sector and eventually work towards improving it.

Public Relations Disasters

The BP oil spill that occurred in May 2010 brings to evidence a new challenge companies face in modern times. How to manage an image crisis? The overwhelming exposure to the media and the integrated means of communication can define the corporate image as a competitive advantage or disadvantage in the global economy. The overall perception of a brand affects the company's share price, funding availability, business alliances and ultimately its success. I believe this is a current topic with great impact on business management. If I could create a Wharton course, it would be called "Image Crisis: How to Manage It".

Currently I work for the largest private bank in Latin America and due to its magnitude it is clear to me its responsibility towards all different layers of Brazilian society and economy, from the individuals to the companies, from the governments to the industries. I value the high ethical and moral standards Itau has set for itself along its history and the effort the high management of the group makes to pass on this culture to every single employee. This is how Itau's image was built.

The 2008 crisis made these admirable values of Itau stand out. At the time, I was working at the derivative sales desk and, like in many other economies, Brazilian companies were taking advantage of the economic *bonanza* to leverage their balance sheets through derivatives instruments. Many of these companies reported a series of outstanding results because of these transactions. However, when the crisis hit hard the entire globe, these same instruments were classified as "toxic derivatives" and the companies were no longer willing to take responsibilities for their choices.

For Itau it was a crisis within the crisis. To have the brand associated with irresponsible sales of high risk instruments was unacceptable. A deep investigation was conducted to determine whether Itau had been diligent in conducting business. I was part of a group responsible for checking if the clients had been warned of all the risks and possible downturns of the deals. In the end of the investigation my team proved that it had been the clients' decision to take such risks and that Itau had acted responsibly and following compliance and suitability rules. On the other hand, other Brazilian financial institutions could not attest they cared the same way for clients and consequently their business was hurt and their images to the general public was of negligent management that allowed dishonest behavior from employees. This is an example of image crisis management and how it can launch a company to success or bury it in failure.

Another good illustration of the topic is the comments and attitudes of Mr. Tony Hayward, former BP's CEO, after the oil spill disaster. BP's image was already extremely fragile after the incident. However Mr. Hayward managed to undermine it even more in two different occasions. First by making an insensitive statement after the spill had occurred saying "I'd like my life back", disregarding the affected lives of thousands of people who had lost so much and were suffering the consequences of the spill as well as the damages caused to marine and wildlife habitats. The second public relations gaffe committed by Mr. Hayward was to attend a yatch race in the middle of the BP crisis. It was not considered the adequate attitude of a leader during a grieving period and it raised more criticism and attacks to the image of the company. These two simple attitudes hurt BP's recovery plans and culminated in Mr. Hayward's resignation - clear examples of lack of awareness of the consequences of one's act over a company's image.

The skills to manage image crises are imperative nowadays, as no company or brand is free from suffering unexpected tragedies or undergoing investigations regarding the way business is conducted. I would personally contribute to the creation of this new course with my experience in handling a potential image crisis in Itau during the 2008 crisis. As Wharton already has remarkable courses teaching students to adopt a responsible approach towards business, I believe such course would fit in the school's strong curriculum complementing already existing ones such as 'Strategic Brand Management', 'Risk and Crisis Management', 'Executive Leadership' and 'Global Strategic Management'.

Social Impact at the Core of Business

In addition to increasing investments in social impact activities, companies have been increasing social efforts' link to their core businesses. From having leaders trained by building popular houses as Accor does in Chile, to formatting entire cities according to sustainable values as Vale does in Brazil, companies have been striving to find ways of making social benefits a natural consequence of their regular business activities. As a result, the new generation of leaders will have to be prepared not only to run successful businesses, but also to read society and optimize companies' social impact by leveraging existent business activities.

Wharton is already acting to prepare its students for this enhanced leadership role. Last year it saw the launch of an experimental course entitled "Social Impact and Responsibility: Foundations", aimed at providing theories and case studies of social impact activities in the private sector. Because I believe in the importance of this subject and of "hands on" application, I would create an additional elective course to give students the opportunity to face a real challenge of generating social impact.

The course I suggest would be called "Social Impact and Responsibility: Undergoing a Real Challenge" and would give students an opportunity to put theory into practice. The new course would require the "Social Impact and Responsibility: Foundations" course as background, and would have two components: strategy and experience.

The first component would consist of a group project focused on developing a social impact strategy and implementation plan for a real company. Students would have to respect a budget defined by the company in order to guarantee the strategy's financial feasibility. In the end of the course, each group would present its project to the firm's management team, being students' final course evaluation linked to feedback received from the same firms. This first component of the course would be modeled after the Wharton Global Consulting Practicum, which already bridges campus activities with real companies.

The second component of the course would consist of a trip abroad to visit a company that already has positive social impact embedded in its activities. This trip would happen in partnership with already existent international courses in Wharton, like the GIP, the Wharton International Volunteer Program or the Lauder dual-degree, in order to leverage their trip organization expertise.

The course would achieve several objectives. First and foremost, it would allow students to truly experience the challenge of creating a feasible social impact strategy.

Second, this course would allow students to practice aspects learned in other Wharton courses, such as teamwork, leadership, presentation skills and structured and pragmatic approach to challenges. In addition, it would be an extra source of summer and full-time job offers for students, since they could be invited to implement the project developed during classes.

Combined, both "Social Impact and Responsibility" courses would give students a sound base to their social impact business education: theory in the "Foundations" course and a practical application in the "Undergoing a Real Challenge" course.

I believe this course has great potential for success, and course success would mean benefits for both school and students. For Wharton, preparing leaders to generate profits together with positive social impact is not only a strategic need, but an opportunity to consolidate itself as a strong player in growing social impact business space. For students, hands on experience in a topic of growing importance to the business world will give them a unique competitive advantage and a chance to connect with their classmates through a challenging and rewarding experience.

Finally, working on the implementation of this course would mean for me a way of gaining more experience in a subject of my interest and also a way of starting to contribute with Wharton-Lauder community, in retribution to all that it has already been doing for me through so many informal conversations with students and alumni and through Wharton Latin American Student Association's support for my application.

Cultural Sensitivity When Conducting Business

One of my favorite undergraduate classes at Penn was a class on Terrorism by Professor Gale. I grew up on Tom Clancy novels, sneaking them out of my mom's purse before she went to work when I was twelve. His books were equally captivating and terrifying with their current events-like theme. Professor Gale's class was an intellectual attempt to understand an often ill-defined and politically charged topic. Since leaving Penn, I have encountered many stereotypes and ill-conceived notions associated with Latin America. From the Managing Director that takes a connecting flight through Houston to Mexico City with Continental because he doesn't trust Aeromexico's direct flight to the exchange students in Argentina and Spain that won't eat meat because they are afraid of Mad Cow disease; misunderstandings about Latin America abound and do not seem to be abating. In my experience such cultural biases are inefficient and stymie the execution of cross-border transactions.

My proposal for a new Wharton course topic would be to tailor a class that addresses the existence of cultural biases in a business setting and how to effectively manage them. I would also push to make this class part of the Wharton core-curriculum in order to reinforce the idea that the art of conducting business in any environment is not simply numbers driven. In fact, my course could be just one of many classes offered that satisfy a new general requirement titled *Conducting Business in an Emerging Market*. Other classes could analyze the style of business and negotiation in other regions of the world such as India, Asia or the Middle East.

Like one of the episodes on the hit show "Diary" by MTV, my specific class would be titled "Latin America – you think you know but you have no idea". Topics for class discussion could be pulled from my experiences, where I witnessed first-hand how all parties involved tended to exhibit a general amount of ignorance. When it comes to understanding each other Latin Americans and Americans alike seem to view each other through stereotypical lenses that bias their judgment and negatively impact their ability to conduct business. Americans tend to view Latin Americans as belonging to less developed nations with cheap currencies and inferior services. Latin Americans tend to view Americans as the proverbial "gringo" that does not understand that he is no longer in America. In fact, developing the right business strategy is useless unless you can relate to the client on his terms and present the proposal in a manner that is conducive to a productive relationship, which requires an understanding of the client's cultural biases.

While at Penn I majored in Hispanic studies in conjunction with my degree in international studies and business. The professors I met and the classroom discussions we had as part of my Hispanic studies major were the most critical to helping me successfully conduct business in Latin America. One such class was with a recognized Professor who was dedicated to Latin American literature of the 20th century. As part of classroom discussion we analyzed stereotypes associated with gender and Latin culture. The discussions piqued my curiosity and drove me to write my senior thesis about the gender biases linked to the Latin American male with said Professor as my adviser. In my thesis I traced the formation of certain stereotypes to past events and their impact by using my own heritage as a case study. I discovered later at the Bank that a better understanding of such cultural biases and their formation actually helped me in my interactions with clients. My class would attempt to cull the various classroom discussions I had as part of my Hispanic studies major and distill the salient points relevant for understanding cultural biases in Latin America.

I believe people today are increasingly called upon to work or even live internationally as part of their normal job description. Developing a curriculum that reflects the changing work environment will simply help to better prepare Wharton graduates for the challenges of tomorrow. By leveraging the diversity already present at Penn's campus students could really dive deep into the nitty-gritty of how people think and make decisions in different cultures. That way when Matt from Indiana is asked by General Mills to lead the negotiations for a brand licensing agreement with a local distributor in Mexico City, Matt will know not to take a taxi off the street from the airport that many of the actual negotiations will be conducted over long lunches with ample amounts of tequila and wine and that a heartfelt toast to the health of his family's counterpart could actually go a long way in establishing a strong work relationship.

Asian Media

Michael Jackson, Madonna, Eminem, Usher,
Britney Spears, Avatar, Terminator, Batman, Spiderman

Do you recognize above mentioned musicians, movies, and comic books?
How about below? Do any of them ring a bell?

Girl Generation, Wonder Girls, BoA,
TaeGukGi: Brotherhood Of War, The Host, Old Boy, Dooly

They are the most famous musicians, movies and comic book characters in Korea. I bet you did not recognize most of them. This triggers a unique idea in me for a new Wharton course.

New Wharton Course

I would like to create Wharton course called *'Globalization of Asian Media and Entertainment Contents'* in conjunction with Wharton's signature program – *Global Immersion Program (GIP)*. The course will explore various issues faced by Asian Media &Entertainment (M&E) firms in their globalization efforts in order to develop effective global strategies and associated marketing plans on their behalf.

Motivation

As a global citizen born in Korea, raised in Thailand, and educated in the U.S., I have been questioning how I can share great Asian cultural contents with all my friends around the world. For instance, from the late '90s, *'Hanryu (Korean Fever)'* swept across China, Thailand, Malaysia, Philippines and many more as Korean M&E contents, including music, TV drama, and movies, have gained great popularity among Asian nations. Many attempts have been made by Korean M&E companies and entrepreneurs to penetrate into the western markets but *'Hanryu'* stops at the border of the Orient. Some argue that it is due to the language and cultural barriers. But I disagree given the worldwide success of the movie *'Crouching Tiger, Hidden Dragon'* whose cast was all Asian and dialogues were in Chinese with English subtitle. Through media sector screening strategy project and pre-post merger integration project of two largest Korean multi program providers while working at McBain, I realized the problem needs a holistic approach of strategy, marketing, and finance.

Ideal course structure and teaching method

Students will begin the course during summer/winter breaks in conjunction with the Wharton GIP. Students will tour Asian regions and meet with top executives in Asian M&E industry such as *Jinyoung Park (CEO of JYP Entertainment)* and *Sooman Lee (CEO of SM Entertainment)* to gain first-hand insights and experiences of their globalization efforts and difficulties that they face. On-campus, the course will coordinate with Wharton Media & Entertainment Club to co-host the premier MBA M&E conferences and invite guest speakers like *Matthew C. Blank (W'72, CEO of Showtime Network)*, to share the latest trends in global M&E industry with students.

During the course, students will be divided into small groups and select an Asian country to research and analyze its M&E industry, global appeals and strengths of its cultural contents. Students will be provided with necessary academic and industry fundamentals through in-class lectures and diverse academic disciplines of Wharton in order to formulate their key findings and insights into practical solutions for Asian M&E companies.

At the end, the course will invite top executives in M&E industry like *Warren N. Lieberfarb (W'65, ex- President of Warner Home Video)* and *Brian L. Roberts (W'81, CEO of Comcast Corporation)* to serve as judges while students act as the CEO of Asian M&E firm and present their global strategies and associated marketing plans. The winning team will receive a chance to present their ideas to CEOs of Asian M&E companies that they met during the Wharton GIP.

Impact of the new course and my contribution

Students will gain diversified cultural and in-depth industry experiences and have the first-hand opportunity to apply the concepts, tools, theories and paradigms they learned in their classes to solve real-time business problems faced by Asian M&E companies. For those who are interested in M&E career, the course will provide them with deeper understanding of oriental cultures. Regional network and insights gained in the course could be utilized to discover variety of unique cultural contents with global appeal during their M&E career. By doing so, they will not only generate opportunities for significant economic value to many Asian countries, but also play an integral part in raising global standard of living by diversifying cultural contents that global citizens can enjoy.

My abilities in analytical techniques and developing new business strategies will be a valuable asset to the course development. The in-depth market research and benchmarking materials on Asian and global M&E markets that I developed during my recent M&E related projects can be used in leading class discussions. Also, I can provide vivid pictures of Korean and Asian M&E industries that are very different from the West by sharing my project experiences in class. In addition, I believe my personal and professional network in Asia will come in handy when I try to connect to the research targets with my classmates.

Investing in Education

The current recession has exacerbated fiscal deficits at all levels of America's government, impacting key services including education. Fiscal year 2011 shortfalls for 46 states totaled $121 billion, or 19 percent of their total budgets, a deficit that would be even larger without federal assistance. With limited improvements to the fiscal situation on the horizon, America will have to live on a tighter budget. Currently, state and local governments fund over 90% of K-12 school funding. Unfortunately, within these future spending cuts, educational budgets will not be spared.

For many public schools that are already underfunded, their predicament will continue to worsen and further contribute to American students lagging behind their global peers. Since 2000, the Organization for Economic Co-operation and Development has administered the Program for International Student Assessment ("PISA") test to compare academic performance among 15-year-old students from member countries; the U.S. students have consistently under performed in every sample. The latest PISA results in 2006 highlighted that U.S. students scored below the average combined score for both science and mathematics literacy. America's education system faces the daunting challenge of improving its performance of preparing students to compete in an increasingly globalized world with less funding.

Within Wharton's Business and Public Policy Department, I would create a course to reduce educational costs while improving student outcomes: "Investing in Education." The course's primary objective would be to focus on maximizing returns on K-12 education spending. In partnership with University of Pennsylvania's Graduate School of Education ("GSE"), the class would search for and analyze the most efficient solutions to systemic problems within America's school system. Leveraging the expertise of the GSE's Policy, Measurement and Evaluation Division, the course would apply an investor's mentality to capital allocation by focusing on generating the greatest educational returns.

"Investing in Education" would harness the diverse backgrounds of Wharton students to provide the business acumen necessary for such a massive endeavor. Course participants could utilize their unique perspectives to help tackle the fiscal constraints confronting policy makers and school administrators within a strained budgetary environment. For example, my background as an M&A investment banker developed my ability to find untapped synergies within a large scale organization. As an institutional investor, my conversations with the leaders of restructuring companies have taught me the importance of transforming the culture of an organization in order to implement real change. Combined with the operational, marketing and entrepreneurial know-how of classmates, the course would apply a direct focus on return on capital in its evaluation of the effectiveness of current educational reforms and their potential to be applied on a national scale.

The course would undergo a deep-dive analysis of the three most-promising avenues for improvement: Performance-based incentive programs for teachers, methods of incorporating technology in the classroom and different models of charter schools, such as the Philadelphia Mastery Charter Schools. Students would evaluate current reform movements and develop innovative solutions to improve upon these efforts. The course would invite guest lecturers on the front-line of educational reform to share their insights on the obstacles that have confronted them. For example, leaders of initiatives such as the Common Core State Standards and Open Educational Resources movement could be invited to join a discussion panel along with the Association of American Publishers, the lobbying group of educational publishers, to highlight the financial and educational benefits of digitalizing America's schools. By also addressing the pros and cons of each potential solution, discussion panels would also provide an opportunity for students to understand how to develop consensus among parties with different objectives.

"Investing in Education" would provide a forum for Wharton students to make a difference with their talents and supplement their existing coursework. The class of future business leaders would gain experience in negotiating with different parties for a common goal, reforming bureaucratic institutions and generating higher returns from lower investments in capital. More importantly, the students would learn what is required to be champions of innovation. The course could motivate fellow classmates to pursue summer internships and full-time jobs within the education space. "Investing in Education" would raise awareness of the fiscal threat to one of the country's most vital assets and could help bring additional reform required by America's school.

Private Sector Principles for Public Sector Impact

A recent area of interest in business concerns lessons the private sector can impart to the social sector. While much has advanced, what is needed is a synthesis of the best practices developed by the business and academic communities. A coherent presentation of private sector practices in the social sector, including outcomes and pitfalls, would do much to advance the discourse for students at Wharton. A course entitled, "What Profitability Means to Nonprofits: Private Sector Principles and the Social Sector," would bring Wharton's strengths to bear and present students with a means of incorporating social impact in their careers.

This course would not only provide a powerful way to apprise Wharton students of professional opportunities, but would provide rigorous training to tackle the toughest problems in the social sector. In my career, I have seen business professionals struggle to identify how to best apply their skills to contribute and have social impact. I first experienced the difficulties of using private sector approaches when I advised venture philanthropies and foundations in England. These foundations sought to lower the high 22% poverty rate among children in the UK, and wanted measurable results. Unlike the private sector, where a simple rate of return would suffice, there was a variety of opinion and even seasoned professionals had difficulty determining the right approach.

Among my peers and students I have spoken to at Wharton, there lacks certainty about the best way to be involved in social impact. The options are unclear and the fields are many, from international development to domestic social causes and domestic economic revitalization. Most importantly, business professionals seek the most effective interventions and quantifiable impacts.

This course would include business planning for nonprofits and inform students of powerful private-public partnerships. While business plans for nonprofits were previously unheard of, now they are a prerequisite to funding. Many influential nonprofit organizations and foundations are closely linked to for-profit companies. Microsoft and the Gates Foundation, for example, mutually benefit from expert analysis and strategy to drive grant decision-making. The social sector is also lucrative, as demonstrated by the public flotation of SKS microfinance and estimated global demand for microcredit of $250 billion.

Wharton has already made strides in illuminating these links. Course content in microfinance addresses economic development, and dozens of articles on Knowledge@ Wharton concern the social sector, from the role of technology to supply chain management. Furthermore, "Social Wealth Venturing" taught by Ian MacMillan, as well as the Wharton Social Venture Fund, combine analytical rigor with a social focus. Finally, the Global Consulting Practicum is another great forum to use business analytics in solving the toughest problems facing the social sector. "Private Sector Principles and the Social Sector" could connect to these courses and provide an academic underpinning and context.

In my experience, analytical rigor is typically at the core of successful social interventions. This course would review current prominent methods for measuring social outcomes, including developments around the Social Return on Investment (SROI). The class would analyze whether nonprofits should employ Cost-Effectiveness Analysis, where cost per high school graduate is measured, or Cost-Benefit Analysis, to include indirect results, such as lower incarceration and unemployment rates. Other metrics, such as Acumen Fund's BACO methodology, to quantify an investment's social output, and the Theory of Change of nonprofits, would be instrumental in establishing a core understanding of metrics.

A survey of the field by major issue area would clarify for students the sectors they should engage in. Sectors covered would include foundation and nonprofit management, microfinance, social sector consulting, and the role of corporations and corporate social responsibility in the social sector. Case studies on Teach for America, Acumen Fund, the Bridgespan Group, and Nike, would provide students with examples of successful strategies and organizations to analyze.

Wharton is well placed to instruct at the intersection of business and the social sector. This connects with Wharton's three pillars, which include Social Impact, and many Wharton students are already engaged in the social sector. An effective course on business principles and the social sector could be part of the core. With great strides already made by Wharton, this course would be a strong backbone to prepare students and leaders for significant impact.

PART II

LAUDER DUAL DEGREE ESSAYS

DESCRIBE A CHALLENGING CROSS-CULTURAL EXPERIENCE

QUESTION

Describe a cross cultural experience in your adult life that was challenging to you. How did you meet this challenge and what did you learn from the experience? (1,000 words)

INTRODUCTION

The Lauder program at Wharton is a very unique program that is truly one of a kind. It is very well known and highly regarded at Wharton and beyond. A distinctly interdisciplinary program, it is targeted at applicants with significant international experience and interests, particularly if an international career is something they are strongly considering.

Leonard Lauder, the Chairman Emeritus, describes the program as the following: "The program of the Institute is not an academic or intellectual luxury, but rather a business necessity and a national imperative. There truly is a global economy, and we handle the problems and opportunities that international business has created. One good place to start is in our universities, the training arena for tomorrow's managers."

For those students with a passion for international affairs and the background to get into the program (advanced ability in a language is one of the requirements), this program is second to none among top business schools.

Bridging Cultural Ties in Afghanistan

My most challenging cross-cultural experience occurred in Afghanistan, where from November 2009 to June 2010, I led a team. Our mission: convince the local Afghan people to support the Marines' presence in their community, and help fight the Taliban insurgency. It was no small task convincing the highly fragmented, war-weary villages that yet another foreign army from halfway around the world had their best interests at heart. I focused my effort in four main areas: restoring local government, sponsoring village reconstruction projects, reducing the opium harvest funding the Taliban insurgency, and marketing the 'message' of American tolerance of Muslim faith.

The City Council was the only locally-elected government in the war-torn region, and sectarian violence and assassinations had driven most of the council into hiding. By bringing basic governance back to the area, we could restore the region's infrastructure and services. I launched a campaign to win the trust of the villagers and help revive their locally-elected authorities. I authorized increased security patrols to protect their villages, and provided basic medical care to their people. As our team won their trust, I began chairing weekly City Council meetings myself, moderating discussions regarding project proposals and security issues through my interpreter in their native Pashto. As security conditions improved, the City Council members gradually regained their authority, and returned to their traditional role of mediating disputes and leading local solutions. By maintaining the principle of 'Afghan solutions to Afghan problems', the city council regained their self-initiative, rather than relying on Marines to adjudicate their community issues.

Through village reconstruction efforts, our team sponsored small but high profile projects, hiring large numbers of unskilled workers to alleviate the area's estimated 60% unemployment. Our first project - sponsoring locals to dig irrigation canals in their village - seemed simple enough. But we quickly learned that our influence in the region's delicate tribal balance could easily cause community unrest. Days after the project started, we were beset by angry mobs from nearby families downstream from the canals, who accused us of cutting off their access to water. From this incident, we learned the importance of community consensus-building in project vetting, as well as the central role that water played in shaping the area's tribal politics.

Understanding Helmand's underlying economics was critical to explaining our area's social behavior. We knew the Taliban used Helmand's vast poppy harvest to finance their violence, but US forces were forbidden to destroy poppy crops- we had to convince farmers not to grow the poppies in the first place. We asked our trusted elders to explain why devout Muslims grew this 'haraam' (religiously outlawed) plant , and learned that narco-traffickers provided cash advances - generally needed for wedding dowries or funeral expenses - for a farmer's future poppy crop. If the harvest failed, the family was more indebted, and the vicious cycle of poppy dependency was set.

I found that opium was the only area crop that would grow in un-irrigated soil, but I was surprised to learn that raw opium was worth less than what farmers could be earning by growing alternate crops, such as wheat, in the same physical space. By making the connection between cash flow and water scarcity, we actively targeted the poorest and most arid communities that were likely to grow opium. We engaged the villages with day-labor projects to improve irrigation and built wells to increase access to water, and provided cash wages that could be used to cover large family expenses. The next opium harvest in our area was the lowest ever recorded since US troops moved into the area. With enough money to provide for their families, and enough water to grow wheat and other legal crops, farmers declined the services of the loan sharks and broke the cycle of poppy cultivation.

Another cultural challenge to overcome was controlling the 'message' of our military's intentions to the villagers. Local religious elders, or mullahs, had inexplicably rejected our overtures for dialogue and cooperation. Afghans inviting us for tea always remarked their surprise that we were not attempting to convert them to Christianity or Judaism. Our team eventually realized this misconception was the result of Taliban propaganda, which warned villagers that Americans had come to 'take away' Islam.

We struck back with a marketing campaign of our own, and held a large gathering at a mosque near our base for all the mullahs. In attendance was our Navy Muslim chaplain, who not only stunned the audience by reciting the Koran in Arabic from memory, but handed out head wraps and prayer rugs as goodwill gifts for village mosques. Over the next few months, we completed nearly forty mosque renovations and refurbishments with the support of the now-friendly mullahs, and gave the Taliban a great deal of difficulty explaining why the American "crusaders" were so eagerly supporting Islamic culture.

The first lesson I learned from my experience in Afghanistan was that while money and power can influence and buy support, it can't buy genuine friendship and trust - those were only earned through honoring promises and owning up to mistakes. In Afghanistan, earning trust also came through showing vulnerability - removing our helmets and bulletproof vests to drink tea with a farmer in his field made us easy targets, but in the long run, the trust gained from the village meant better security than having stand-off conversations dressed head to toe in armor. Second, we learned the importance of having our Afghan partners feel the power of self-responsibility in solving problems, even if we could have done it faster or more efficiently ourselves. I could not force a community take ownership of a school renovation, for example, unless the villages agreed to protect the facilities from vandals, and felt their children would be safe walking to school by themselves. Despite vastly different cultures, the Afghans and I ultimately shared a similar vision- a safe community, the means to provide for our families, and a brighter future for our children

Adapting to Life in Mumbai

In one year living and working in Mumbai, I learned more about life than in the previous twenty-three. One might think that being Indian-American would have prepared me. After all, I'd spent my summers there as a child; I could speak the language; my skin color was the same. But I learned the truth the hard way: nothing can prepare you for the reality of Mumbai.

I stepped off the plane in Mumbai with confidence. I'd just completed method acting training at the Lee Strasberg Institute in New York. I'd studied the Indian entertainment industry reports cover to cover: PwC's in 2006, and KPMG's in 2007. I knew the startling growth rates, production numbers, and foreign investment levels, and considered it the perfect time to go. Furthermore, I'd backpacked sixty countries and worked with executives of multi-national, multi-billion-dollar companies at McBain. I naively thought that if anyone was prepared to tackle this booming foreign market and find work as an actor – it was I.

Without a formal infrastructure of managers, agents, and casting directors, I set to work on my own. I scoured the Internet to build a database of every production company and media firm in the city. I carefully designed my sales package with resumes on heavy paper, reference letters on NYU letterhead, and hi-resolution comp cards. I braved the heat for days delivering more than a hundred packages – to find the companies did not exist – or to have them permanently filed away at the front desk when they did exist. Countless follow-up phone calls revealed that everyone other than the receptionist was "in a meeting." When I'd finally reach someone, they all oddly had the same question: "Where are you from?" After my answer, their interest fizzled.

For months, each empty lead wore on my spirit. Beyond the professional struggle, I'd been crushed by the basic realities. On the back of my real estate agent's motorcycle, I'd seen fifty apartments before finding one willing to rent to a "foreign bachelor." Changing the word "Secretariat" to "Secretary" on my visa application took six sweaty, bone-crushing trips in the crowded local train. Getting a driver's license took a full-time workweek. Learning to navigate the chaotic zoo of humans, animals, and motor vehicle traffic brought me to my knees. Passing children digging through trash heaps and begging masses of twisted flesh and bone at the intersections brought me to tears. My suburban-American childhood left me unprepared for Mumbai's dark side. After a reality TV celebrity stole my credit card at the gym and emptied my account, I watched police torture him against my pleading – before they took 20,000 rupees out of the recovered money for their efforts.

I remember lying in bed with a viral infection – with no running water, no electricity, and no Internet connection – and crying. Utterly defeated, I turned to my bible of sorts, *Shantaram*, an Australian fugitive's memoir of life in Mumbai's slums. A line I'd read many times before struck me for the first time: *Sometimes you must surrender before you win.* Looking up from rock bottom, I realized that I'd failed to adapt to a new cultural paradigm. Overconfidence and ignorance had led me to use my own strategies instead of learning to work within the system.

I began taking feedback from the city and its people, and adjusted my approach. I realized that in a classist society where perception is everything, I was judged for delivering my own materials – so I hired a courier. Finding professional channels unresponsive, I recognized that business was less qualification and more relationship-based, making my resume and reference letters secondary. I shifted efforts from day to night, sowing countless networking seeds. Most importantly, sensing Bollywood's aversion to outsiders, I began to mask my English with an Indian accent, and adopted uniquely Indian sentence structures and gestures.

In addition to adopting new business strategies, I learned to draw strength from the beauty in this city of contradictions. Afternoons I wasn't auditioning, I tutored children from the local slum under a tree, bringing my guitar to teach music. I learned to appreciate the joys: the first monsoon rain, the brilliant sunsets on the Indian Ocean, and the festivals of Holi and Ganpati, as the rich and poor filled the streets to paint one another or parade massive elephant statues toward the sea. I spoke to the auto-rickshaw drivers, the night watchman, and my favorite waiter. I listened to their stories of hardship and witnessed their infinite generosity, learning gratitude, making simple friendships, and learning to connect with people. The city, and the anger, happiness, and helplessness it brought, were a big part of the renewal of my faith in a higher power.

Networking with my new approach yielded results. Two close friendships – not textbook business strategies – landed me a lead role in an independent feature and helped me transition to the business side, as I joined a London-based production company serving world-class clients. But the new paradigm also brought moral challenges to which I refused to surrender, balancing the need to adapt and the need to retain my identity. In a culture of "gifts" and "favors," I made enemies when I resisted unwelcome advances from India's leading designer. Unwavering, I avoided the ever-present drug use, balancing social integration with my beliefs.

Mumbai taught me a lot. I learned to love her for all her joys and sorrows. Above all, I learned the importance of adapting a strategy to fit a culture. I learned the value of patience and the value of an alternative way. I learned about human nature in a world of desperation. I learned whom to trust and keep close while I rapidly expanded my network to include key figures in the city. I've come to see my Indian-American identity in a more nuanced way, realizing that assimilating and adapting was more difficult than I'd ever imagined, despite my Indian genes. But most importantly, I learned whom I was, what I stood for, and that I had only begun to explore the limits of my tenacity until living and working in Mumbai.

Making It in a Small Town in Bolivia

I come from a family of teachers. My father is a professor, and so is my mother. My paternal grandparents were both teachers, as were their parents. When it came time for me to teach, I may have had the right genes, but I had little experience.

I taught violin for a summer in a small village, in the hills of Bolivia. Traveling to the village was an ordeal. It took six hours by chicken bus to get to the local town and then another hour on the back of a motorcycle taxi to arrive in the village. There was no electricity or running water – drinking water was pumped from a well and set out in the hot sun for days, disinfecting it naturally. I lived on the grounds of a Franciscan missionary, with a German priest and nun to keep me company. I had come to the village alone and nobody spoke English in the town of 4000 people.

My violin students were young children who played instruments crafted by highly skilled local artisans. The children often spoke little Spanish, preferring to use their native tongue, Guarayo.

With few distractions in their day-to-day lives, the violin was often the children's only outlet – perhaps their musical talents could be a ticket out of the village to a different world that they had only witnessed by watching action movies shown nightly on the only village television (powered by a loud humming generator).

It was in this setting that I began to learn the fundamentals of teaching. For 5 to 6 hours a day I taught a variety of classes, ranging from private lessons to classes of 10-12 children. They were hard working. They eagerly awaited each lesson and rapidly demonstrated improvement – any teacher's dream come true.

However, communication was difficult. We spoke to one another in Spanish, a language that was foreign to both of us. For example, when playing in groups, students often rushed the tempo. In an attempt to correct for this, I devoted a class to the importance of timing. No matter how hard I tried, I could not seem to get the message across. "Estás acelerando, estás acelerando!" I would say to no avail. The children looked back at me with blank stares. It took me about half of the class period to realize that none of my students recognized the word "acelerando."

I was in a difficult spot. Not only was I an inexperienced teacher, but communicating ideas was proving to be tough. How could I teach if I couldn't communicate?

I quickly learned that when teaching music, spoken language is not entirely necessary. Music is a form of communication in and of itself, and often the best way to teach is through example. I played my violin alongside my students, often demonstrating the errors through repetition and exaggeration so as to stress the aspect that needed to be changed. In addition to this, I began teaching the children music theory.

The summer was eye opening for me in many ways. It was incredible to feel like a legitimate participant in the culture. Like anyone else in the town, I bathed in the river and used candles to read at night before falling asleep. I ate my meals with the nun and priest and learned of their fascinating experience, having arrived as missionaries in the jungle village 20 years earlier. While I was there, it was clear to me that the town revolved around the church – a testament to the hard work and success of the nun and priest.

My students continued to progress in their studies and by the end of my stay, I organized a group ensemble to perform the Bach Double for some visiting priests. The students and I were pleased with the performance, and it seemed that the priests enjoyed themselves as well. I left the village with more confidence in my competence to teach and my ability to overcome language barriers. By the end of the summer, all of my students understood the word *"acelerando."*

Brazilian in New York

McBain provided me with a challenging and enriching cross-cultural experience last year when it sent me to the US as an expatriate for one semester. I surpassed some of my limits, amplified my vision of the world and its opportunities, and coped with the challenge of my first professional task outside Brazil. I had travelled a lot already for tourism and language studies, but working abroad was totally different because of the responsibilities and performance it demanded. For the first time I was not protected by the handicap label "foreigner" – I had to perform like any other associate in the McBain New York office.

I had entered McBain one year and a half before, straight from college, and, although performing well in McBain Sao Paulo and being recommended to work as an expatriate, I still was not sure I was able to keep an above average performance when working abroad. I was certain, however, that the experience would be worth: choosing the hardest paths has always generated greater experiences and learning, and this time it would not be different.

My first concrete challenge was entering an on-going project and having as a first meeting a discussion with twelve McBainers and clients from various parts of the world about a specific banking subject I had never heard of. Although I did not understand much during the meeting, the subject became clear right after a team mate explained it to me, but it took me a week to get used to all the different accents and idioms and to finally conduct discussions in a proper way. This first challenge provided me with more gains than I expected: besides improving my English, I improved my ability to express myself in Portuguese by incorporating the American way of structuring ideas to the Brazilian one I was used to.

Another important challenge was finding the right fit between my behavior and expectations and the many cultures in my teams. I spent a few weeks telling jokes and personal stories that were either too timid or too exaggerated and listening to stories and comments that made me quite embarrassed, until I found the right level of humor and intimacy. I learned, for example, that irony was very funny for Americans and that Russian censure limits, although still respectful, could be much wider than the ones I was used to. My team had a very nice way of dealing with potentially embarrassing moments though. For example, whenever one of us said something strange, we would laugh, no matter how serious the moment was, and these episodes gradually became a source of good stories for a team that was finding more and more pleasure in spending time together.

I participated in three different teams in the US and the fact that two of them were part of a bigger global post-merger integration team just increased the number of different people and cultures I got in touch with. My teams showed me that different cultures generate different professional environments: Latin American teams were extremely informal while Japanese teams valued hierarchy; North American teams were encouraged to finish work by 8 pm while Spanish teams were expected to work after hours; teams in Germany expressed themselves pretty straightforward while Brazilians used long and colorful sentences. Nevertheless, I learned that all these cultures and professional environments have their pros and cons we must learn to admire and respect. In this sense, for example, I learned from the Americans to point out even small positive things others do. In Brazil, we do not celebrate small things so much, but since I started doing so my teams have felt valued and stimulated to do even better.

Another important aspect of my working experience abroad is that I took seriously my role as an ambassador of the Brazilian culture. I realized that I was the first Brazilian many clients and McBainers would meet and that I would be responsible for their impression of my country. Therefore, I made efforts to show that Brazil was much more than forests and samba. Once people heard about me and my friends learning other languages, studying and working abroad, and contributing to the society through social impact activities, they changed their perception of Brazil. Since then I have received emails asking about the best dates to come and visit and even some asking for help to come as McBain expatriates to Sao Paulo.

Although challenging in understanding and expressing myself correctly in an international business environment, my experience in the US was successful. As a result, I was sent directly from NYC to Mexico and Switzerland for my following cases. I am also going to be pictured at McBain's recruiting website as an example of McBainer with many international experiences in the early steps of my career.

Working abroad taught me to better read people and environments, be aware of my words, gestures and attitudes, and have an ampler spectrum of behaviors that are consistent with my principles and more adequate to different people and situations. Since then, my positioning with people has improved, as well as my presentation and negotiation skills.

I consider international cross-cultural experiences the most enriching ones because they allow me to learn from the most different people and cooperate with them. International experiences amplify my perception of me and of others and also make me realize how big and diverse the world and the possibilities are, enabling me to set goals with higher amplitude. One word that defines what I see and want in cross-cultural experiences is "MORE".

Being back in Brazil is amazing, especially because I can practice and pass forward everything I have learned, but now that I know how good it is to live abroad in contact with other cultures, I do not want to lose my link with the world. This is one of the reasons I decided to apply to Wharton-Lauder.

Banking in Peru

I joined the Bank's Latin America M&A team straight out of college in 2007. I had requested my staffer at the time to place me in the second wave of training that began in late August, which would allow me to work and meet the rest of the team before training. My second day on the job, my Staffer pulls me into her office and asks me to help our team in Peru that just won a sell-side mandate. The next day I was flying down to Peru for my first real adventure without a clue of what I would be doing.

My family is from Latin America – Argentina and Chile to be specific. I have spent many family reunions in one of the two countries as well as a summer abroad in Buenos Aires and a semester abroad in Barcelona, Spain. However, nothing prepared me for what awaited in Peru. I quickly realized that the hardest part of this deal was the fact that I was completely isolated. I had no friends in Lima; I had never met nor worked with the Bank's people in the local office. Worst of all, the months of July and August are constantly overcast, cloudy and rainy, which did not sit well with this Florida resident! After the initial excitement of flying business class to a country I'd never visited wore off, I really felt alone. Not only did I feel alone, but I also felt useless. I will never forget my first two days in Lima as my Bank's colleagues were occupied on other tasks and did not have time to brief me on the transaction or what was expected of me.

I ended up living in the Sheraton hotel and working in Peru for slightly over a month and can honestly say that it was one of the best experiences of my life. I overcame this challenge by taking an interest in and learning about the Peruvian culture. I befriended the Bank's local analysts who took me out on weekends and introduced me to their friends. On our 7 hour bus trips with investors into the jungle to diligence the assets owned by the company I talked with the investors and learned about their companies, objectives and concerns regarding Peru, which I made sure management addressed later in follow-up meetings. During my free time I wandered Lima, learning about the city, its rich history and its culture. I also discovered that Peru has an amazing selection of restaurants with a cuisine that absolutely shocked me! By taking an interest in the culture and the people around me I was able to overcome this challenge.

What my experience taught me is that we live in a big world full of diverse peoples with a variety of interests. I was surprised when one of the bidders that we took to diligence was from Norway and shocked when they ended up winning the asset. It puzzled me that a company in Norway saw value in owning and operating an asset in Peru. But that company had a deep commitment to Latin America, and I noticed early on in my conversations with one of the owners of the company a deep fondness for Peru's culture as well!

Not only did the experience broaden my understanding of business in an international setting, but I also became a huge fan of the Peruvian culture, particularly their food and art. From a local artist I bought three oil paintings that are prominently hung in my apartment. I also discovered that the restaurant *Rafael* has the most delicious grilled octopus and that Peru is renowned for some of the best *ceviches*. I also count the local analysts as some of my closest friends, often dining together. From my conversations with them I learned about the local politics and the history of foreign migration and investment, particularly from the Japanese. I also learned about their quarrels with neighboring countries and how Peru has sometimes shunned investments from its neighbors. What my experience really showed me is that it is impossible to understand what motivates a person from a different country (like our client's management for example) unless you begin with the people and learn about the culture they represent.

Days later, just before I was set to fly out a massive 7.0 earthquake struck Peru. As a testament to the relationship one builds in business, investors I'd met during the diligence process called me to make sure I and everyone in the company were ok and asked me to stay and ascertain what was happening on the ground. Though living and working in Peru was challenging, I succeeded. Months later as everyone seemed to be losing their jobs, I was kept on. My performance in Peru showed my superiors I had what it took to succeed in business and effectively lead transactions. More importantly, what my experience really gave me was a purpose; a desire to use my abilities to help small and medium sized businesses in countries like Peru and Mexico grow, fostering job creation and economic prosperity.

Succeeding as a Woman Working in Mexico

My greatest cross-cultural challenge has been managing the stigma associated with being a professional woman in Mexico. The female factor never impacted the quality of the professional opportunities I had, but it exposed many inhibiting cultural barriers. At the very minimum, these barriers affect women's desire to enter and remain in the professional workforce. But I believe this problem is a significant limiting factor to Mexico's ability to increase its highly skilled workforce, thus limiting the country's ability to grow into a major world business center.

The widespread cultural belief in elitist Mexico is that a woman does not work once she is married, unless it is economically required of her. Otherwise in the eyes of society, it could be misconstrued as her husband lacking the funds to support her; the family's carefully managed image would be tarnished. While many Mexican women do work, there are very few who commit to more than a few years after college graduation. Even fewer advance to senior positions, and virtually none of those are women with children, representing a significant lack of role models. It is challenging to be in that environment when it appears impossible to manage both a family and a career.

The main challenge at work was the light-hearted attitude towards inappropriate comments about women, which I unknowingly condoned for a long time. In a culture where political incorrectness is acceptable, the men in the office often joked about women, or made inappropriate comments on any number of topics. As an open-minded person who can appreciate the jokes, I often found myself ignoring them, or worse, laughing. This caused a vicious cycle – the more I laughed at their women jokes, the more they told. I became "one of the guys" in an environment dominated by men – something I had aspired to in order to fit in at an office far from my support network of family and friends in the US.

Shortly after I had earned what I believed was my male coworkers' respect, I was appointed the Program Coordinator for the Women at McBain initiative in Mexico City. I worked with the female HR Director, the sole female manager, and a senior female partner from McBain's Atlanta office to determine our local women's recruiting and retention strategies. I learned how to appeal to men's business sense to drive the initiatives through. Hypothetically, if we could attract an equal number of women applicants to our firm, we would have double the applicant pool and inevitably, the ability to choose the most talented people, male or female, to work for us. For the women already in our company, we needed to be attentive to their fundamentally different lifestyle requirements and different ways of thinking in order to promote them up through the organization instead of losing them when it appeared impossible to balance family life with a career. We discovered that it just takes a few female role models to give the initiatives some inertia.

When I began organizing the brown bag discussion with a female Mexican CEO for the end of this year, I met with unexpected resistance and skepticism from the male managers. I understood then that their jokes were an expression of the reality, and realized just how little they actually respected my female peers and me. I struggled to grasp this realization; I seemed to get along well with my male colleagues and I had proven myself as a capable analyst. I didn't see any gender barriers, but they still did. I further differentiated myself as the woman who previously facilitated a relaxed environment, in their minds, but now complicated their lives by reprimanding their jokes and requiring that their female team members be excused during the work day to attend women's professional development events. I had to elevate several issues to the HR Director, which aggravated them even more.

An even greater challenge is that many Mexican women also hold similar beliefs, restricting their own progress. They fully expect to go to college, maybe graduate, and then possibly work to pass the time until becoming housewives. While this can be admirable if it's truly what they want, I don't believe it's acceptable to squelch other aspirations because an elitist expectation of a certain image takes precedence. I personally admire those women who have successful careers and who have attained a certain status as a result. On the contrary, I find it challenging to admire the women who have given up their dreams for nothing more than an image. I am even more disappointed that they haven't realized that they can preserve this image while also pursuing their dreams.

Upon making the connection that the vast majority of my coworkers' wives fell into this category, which was likely contributing to the unfortunate attitudes their husbands possessed, I decided it was important to involve them in the Women at McBain initiative. I suggested we invite them to the female CEO presentation. Somewhat surprisingly, many of the wives have accepted graciously, inquiring about the topics of discussion and requesting to extend the time allotted for questions. While not expecting any of them to start job hunting immediately after the event, I believe that we have planted the first seed of potential. I learned that it is important for women to have role models, and I am ever more conscious my duty to be one – in Mexico and elsewhere.

Once the men saw how excited their wives were about meeting a female CEO, they became more supportive of the initiative. A few of them apologized to me for their rudeness and resistance, admitting they were wrong. From this, I also learned that it is not only the men's beliefs that must be challenged, but also the women's if society as a whole is to progress. While it will take a while to change my colleagues' beliefs, if that is even possible, we are slowly seeing improvements in their attitudes, resulting in a more collaborative environment for everyone.

WHAT IS YOUR MOTIVATION FOR JOINING THE LAUDER PROGRAM?

QUESTION

Please explain why you are currently applying to Lauder. How do you expect the Lauder joint degree experience to benefit you on both a personal and professional level? (1,000 words)

INTRODUCTION

Given that the Lauder program is a prestigious double degree program at the Wharton School, the Lauder Institute wants to ensure both a suitable professional and cultural match for the tightly knit community. It is designed for people who already have considerable international experience and who intend to maintain an international focus professionally. Those are the themes the Institute generally wants to see in these essays.

The degree seeks not only to provide students with exceptional language ability (advanced language ability is a requirement of the program) but also deep cultural, historical, and social understanding of their region of focus and more globally. The Lauder program can only be done in conjunction with the business school or law school at the University of Pennsylvania. It is possible to be admitted only to the law school or Wharton while not being admitted to Lauder, however the reverse is not possible.

As with all applications, visiting the Lauder Institute and meeting with students and faculty is the only way to get a feel for the program. The community prides itself on being very close and supportive, a feeling that is apparent upon walking through the doors to the Lauder building a few doors down from Huntsman Hall.

Why Lauder #1

In 1998 during my prospective undergraduate school visit, I stumbled upon the Lauder building on the UPenn campus. Reading the foreign-language flyers of business opportunities overseas, and overhearing nearby students discuss their cultural experiences abroad, I felt I had found an academic experience custom-made for me. With naive enthusiasm (and wondering why the program wasn't in the undergraduate brochure), I walked into the admissions office and asked for an application- not realizing Lauder was graduate program. After realizing I was just a high school student, the secretary politely recommended I first obtain a bachelor's degree and a few years of work experience!

Twelve years later, I'm drawn to the same features of Lauder that excited me as that prospective undergrad- an analytically-intense business degree from Wharton to become a better decision-maker, and an international affairs degree to navigate the world through language and cultural training. With a multicultural upbringing, and living over four years of my adult life outside the US, I know that true success in working abroad must come through an ability to communicate culturally and linguistically with the people you are trying to develop relationships with.

While at Georgetown, I immersed myself in the world of foreign policy and deliberately balanced my international affairs major with a business minor, by spending my year abroad in Hong Kong to keep abreast of the rapidly-expanding Chinese economic dominance. Working closely with my South Korean counterparts in their home country during one of the world's largest military exercises allowed me to understand and appreciate the unique cultural mindset of a people living under daily threat from their next-door neighbors. And as a Marine Civil Affairs officer, I received an on-the-job education in Afghan tribal dynamics as we rebuilt a shattered community. The Lauder program represents the next step in my development, by preparing me to work in a foreign country in its host language and culture upon graduation.

Many schools offer weeklong trips to foreign countries and call it a 'global experience'- I want a truly integrated education that will train me to communicate with and relate to foreign cultures in their own language and customs. My experiences abroad only reinforced to me that communicating to someone in their own language, in their own cultural context, is an extraordinarily powerful tool. Whether in China or Afghanistan, I've seen significant change in the other side's attitude once I transition from depending on interpreters to mastering a few phrases in the host nation language. Even when I could only manage a few foreign words, my attempt signified respect and appreciation for my hosts' culture, and they became more open to my message.

As the son of a Quebecois parent, my French-Canadian family environment was my language classroom, nurturing my proficiency in the language even while living in the US. In college, I took high-level French classes to develop my professional communication skills. Although I have not had the opportunity to work in a French-speaking environment through the Marine Corps, I maintain my communication skills and received the highest possible score on the military's French language proficiency test for the past 3 years in a row. But while at ease listening to Québec news via podcast, or conversing with my family members in their colloquial Quebecois dialect, I know that I require more rigorous exposure to Standard French before I can operate in the language professionally. The Lauder program will allow me to develop my French language skills in a business context, and prepare me for a position in overseas consulting or sustainable private equity that requires French with precise fluency.

After four years of reading about international affairs at Georgetown, I decided the best way to understand foreign policy was to see it on the 'front lines'- literally. Joining the Marine Corps enabled me to experience, appreciate, and even take part in headline-making events around the world. But after my tours in Iraq and Afghanistan, I understand there are limits to changing the world while wearing a military uniform. The development work I achieved in Afghanistan as a Civil Affairs officer was immensely rewarding, but I realize the long-term success or failure of similar troubled regions lies not through military force, but through economic development. If I could achieve significant gains in improving the lives and infrastructure of an Afghan community for a few hundred thousand dollars, I can only imagine the social benefit I could accomplish in developing nations, working in firms like E+Co or BP Solar, through responsible and sustainable investments in alternative energy.

In my discussions with Lauder students, I've seen how the intimate class size provides a tight-knit community of diverse-minded people from literally all over the world to collaborate with. This global network will allow me, post-MBA, to pursue the kinds of goals I love the most: like my former colleagues and Lauder students Amy Cheng and Matt Axelrod, I will work abroad, collaborating with people from foreign countries, across different languages and cultures.

Developing my language proficiency through Lauder will open doors to career opportunities unavailable to many of my MBA peers. I feel Lauder is the perfect place for my combination of language ability and career goals. Meeting French track students like Jeremiah Marble and Kathleen Bellehumeur during my school visit, and following their adventures throughout their time at Lauder, has reinforced my interest in the program. Their research in the Senegalese solar power market, published in the 2010 Lauder Global Business Insights Report, is exactly the kind of work I envision doing with a Lauder degree, and further proof to me that Lauder is the right place to start my post-military career.

Working in Afghanistan proved to me that I can succeed in a challenging foreign environment and overcome significant cultural obstacles. My communication, language, and business skills that I will develop through Wharton and Lauder will further demonstrate to firms that I can thrive in any corner of the globe.

Why Lauder #2

When I stumbled upon the new Hindi track at Lauder while researching MBA programs, I felt as if it had been created just for me. With high expectations, I spent a sunny November day interacting with Lauder faculty and students and attending Professor Guillen's class. As I left the campus, I was absolutely certain; it was exactly where I want to spend the next two years of my life.

I am currently applying to Lauder to put myself in the best possible position to pursue my goal of working in management in the international M&E industry. I plan to take full advantage of every aspect of the experience: the formal and informal education, language instruction, summer immersion, research, community, and network. After working at McBain, acting in Mumbai, and creating content for world markets as a production manager in London, I feel truly ready for the Wharton/Lauder experience. To reach my next goal of an entry-level management position at a top company, the Wharton MBA will be essential; then working towards an international management role, the Lauder education will be invaluable. To be successful working internationally, particularly in India, I must learn more about the country and the language, fill gaps in my business knowledge, brush up on fundamentals, and formally study international management.

I expect the Wharton/Lauder joint-degree experience to benefit me on a professional level first by preparing me for the challenges I am certain to face in international management, and then helping open the doors to opportunities to tackle those challenges. Between the Lauder-specific classes, the MBA/MA joint courses, and the non-MBA electives, and the accompanying cases, class discussions, faculty lectures, and projects, I will build my confidence and knowledge in international management and global context. I will use the in-country experience and language instruction over the next two years to perfect the language and country skills that will be critical to my professional success in India. The joint degree and Lauder's reputation for educating international leaders will open doors and serve as a signal to employers, putting me ahead of my competition. From the prominent business and political leaders I'll meet during the summer immersion, to my classmates in the program, to the Lauder-specific guest speakers, to the Lauder alumni around the world, I will grow and leverage my network to find career opportunities and potentially even generate business in the future.

Professionally, I am applying to the Hindi track because I want to be relied on as a trusted liaison between India and the world's great companies who want to do business there. I want to be fluent in India; I've learned firsthand how important it is not to be viewed as an outsider. Additionally, Wharton's unparalleled reputation in India reinforces why Wharton/Lauder is the best next step. From my earliest memories, I've been traveling to India; it is a happy coincidence that it has since grown to become a main stage for the next economic act. From the fundamentals, I am convinced that the future lies there: its billion-strong consumer base is growing quickly, English is prevalent, it boasts countless highly educated graduates, and it is a functioning democracy. But it is not all roses. A trip through China, its future rival, highlighted its shortcomings: inadequate infrastructure, regionalism, corruption, and crushing poverty. As a business leader, these social issues will always factor in my decision-making. Beyond a direct revenue impact, studying the history and culture will enhance my appreciation for the subtleties and enrich my experiences, in dealings with board members to employees from different corners of India, a country of 22 official languages and 3000 years of history.

I expect the Wharton/Lauder joint-degree experience to benefit me on a personal level by deepening my understanding of our world, fulfilling my intellectual curiosity, and connecting me to a community of truly global people. Nearly every dollar I save and day of vacation I accumulate goes towards exploring our world. Since high school, I've dedicated myself to this cause, backpacking and photographing 60 countries, and filling notebook after notebook with my adventures. Subscribing to the "when in Rome" philosophy, I've found myself eating maize cakes and sun-dried fish in a Nairobi tenement, and sleeping on the floor beside my local hosts in Phnom Penh. Reading back on my notebooks of observations and conversations, I see themes of business, politics, infrastructure, culture, and history. These notebooks have helped me develop a lens with which to view our world, and the ability to note common themes and fundamental differences in places and their people.

Beyond the intellectual stimulation, I look forward to the sense of community, a vital aspect to me in choosing an MBA program. From the energy I felt at Lauder, I most look forward to meeting my international and multi-lingual classmates and learning as much from them as from the exciting curriculum, like Professor Guillen's Amazing Race class. Having classmates with backgrounds beyond the typical MBA realm, be it from International Development and Public Policy, will make for far more holistic discussions. Furthermore, I understand and value the unique perspective of a foreigner living and working in a different culture. I will soak up lessons from my classmates, whether an American Russian speaker or a German working in Saudi Arabia. This give-and-take will make this two-year experience incredibly richer in a way that can't be obviously quantified.

Personally, I am applying to the Hindi track because I want to deepen my understanding of my heritage and language, and maintain a connection to India. I've always been drawn to the country. My interest has shown up in the books on my bedside and the music I listen to. It showed up in my studies, with language classes at the Hindu temple on Sundays, and a minor in Hindi at the University of Michigan. Soon enough, I was living and working in India. Moreover, memories of children my age begging at our window have stayed with me, and one day I hope to effect social change in a country that needs it so desperately, through media or otherwise. On a very personal level, two years of Hindi instruction will finally give me a chance to bring my language skills to that of a native speaker, which will not only allow me to communicate effortlessly with my grandparents, but also to pass the language to my children.

I can't think of a better next step than developing language fluency and obtaining two degrees in two years at the best international business program in the world, along with 50 close friends who will go on to do groundbreaking things in business and politics all over the globe.

Why Lauder #3

I hope to build my career in the Emerging Markets sector of the world economy. Having lived abroad several times in my life and minored in Spanish, I know that on a personal level, I enjoy the prospect of working in another country, preferably in Latin America. I enjoy speaking Spanish, embedding myself into new cultures, and engaging in a society that is different from my own. I value a global perspective.

I view the Lauder program as a conduit to meet other like-minded students who place high value on international experience and international business careers. The program will accomplish two of my important goals: (a) improve my language fluency, and (b) enhance my understanding of an international management environment.

Professionally, the development of business level Spanish skills is essential to my success in an Emerging Markets focused career track. Having lived and studied in Spain, Argentina, Bolivia, and Mexico, my language abilities are sufficient, but I have room for improvement. Recently, I have been taking Spanish lessons. The classes have been very helpful – hopefully my progress will be evident in my most recent OPI test.

Beyond the language focus of the program, I am drawn to the program's focus on international management. Two years ago, I had an opportunity to work on a deal to finance the construction of a toll road in the Philippines. The Philippine government wanted to build a highway from Manila to an outskirt district. The pre-existing road was small, narrow, and increasingly busy – filled with individuals traveling to work and school. However, construction of highways is expensive, and in order to finance a new road, the government turned to my bank to underwrite a bond in the international capital markets.

I was nervous, being the sole analyst on the management team which produced a $150 million structured financing for the construction of the road. From a professional perspective, the execution phase of the deal was quite a learning experience. However, I learned something more important during that due diligence trip to Manila. I learned that it felt good to help manage something that could improve peoples' lives.

Although it was a for-profit undertaking, and we were by no means acting as a group of philanthropists, it was rewarding to know that our work enabled the construction of the road. When complete, the road would provide a means for people to access education, employment, and even emergency healthcare. Simply put, without financing, the road would not be built. It felt satisfying to realize that my team could enable the construction of something that could so dramatically improve the lives of Philippine people.

This eye-opening experience and other transactions like it have pushed me to pursue a career in Emerging Markets. I find the field appealing because sub-investment grade societies have the greatest need for development. More often than not, project finance in the US results in conveniences, profits, and efficiencies (these are all good things). However, project finance in Emerging Market countries more significantly improves living standards, education, and most importantly, healthcare. Having lived in several third world countries, I feel that my background is well tailored for such a career focus.

The Lauder program covers many more bases beyond its advanced business language program. Its focus on international issues and its exchange program guarantee that graduates leave with a strong understanding of how economies interact with each other. With the growth of globalization, business leaders with an international perspective will better orchestrate an efficient global economy. They will ultimately create more jobs and raise living standards while simultaneously avoiding economic pitfalls brought about by faulty leadership.

The Lauder program can also help me understand and appreciate cultural differences. For example, three years ago, I spent several weeks living in Pakistan. I recall my arrival distinctly. The air smelled of smoke from the countless factories nearby and peoples' wood burning stoves. Women were rarely seen out of the house and when they were spotted, they were usually covered from head to toe. The cultural differences were astounding – one occurrence clearly stands out in my mind.

I remember riding in a *tuk tuk* past a large billboard with black paint all over it. Apparently a cell phone company had begun a marketing campaign that featured a pretty girl in a shirt that was considered too low cut for the religious conservatives of the country. A public outcry manifested itself into a smattering of paint over the girl's billboard image. Clearly, the marketing department of that company had not considered cultural norms when creating the ad campaign.

This experience and other similar ones made me realize how different our cultures were. In Pakistan, drinking alcohol is illegal and any kind of display of sex appeal in public is virtually nonexistent. No alcohol means no bars, night life, or socializing. No sex appeal means fewer advertisements in fashion. In fact, it was rare even to see a woman on the streets and even more rare to see her wearing anything other than a plain *shalwar kameez* with a *dupatta*.

The Lauder program offers students the opportunity to study abroad in their target career environments, enabling them to better understand the cultural factors that drive an economy. My experience in Pakistan was a perfect example of the importance of international studies when conducting business activities. While my interests currently reside in Latin America, I believe the same principals apply. My commitment to focus on the Emerging Markets is a commitment to understanding the driving factors behind international business.

Why Lauder #4

My professional objective is to contribute to the combination of profits and positive social impacts in the business sector. My business background, international experiences and social work activities so far have influenced this decision and I expect Wharton-Lauder to prepare me for the task, especially through two aspects: knowledge and people. The joint-degree will allow me to improve my business skills, access ideas and examples of international business activities around social impact and to be part of a community of potential future partners in my activities.

Many countries in the world have been increasing efforts to fight poverty and lack of health, education and culture. In Brazil we are experiencing an economic growth that may soon have a cap if we do not fix base problems, such as lack of skilled working force and of a strong base of consumers, by bringing the poor part of the population onboard of growth and its benefits. Local and international individuals, institutions and companies have, as a result, been investing more money and energy in social activities every year. Aligned with this scenario, my professional plan is to be part of these movements by optimizing their contributions' impacts. Brazil and other countries have a lot to learn from one another, just as social activities have a lot in efficiency to learn from business activities. In this sense, I see myself some years from now working to match financial success with positive social impact in a global social institution such as the World Bank, or in a multinational company that has profits and social impact as part of its mission.

Having always been interested in other countries and cultures, I took an exchange program to the UK during high school and understood that the world was big and full of opportunities. After that I started my French lessons, went for an exchange program in France, and attended two undergraduate courses at the same time in business and international relations - by that time I knew I wanted to play an international leading role and needed to prepare in business skills and in getting in touch with different cultures, histories, models and people. I graduated in business and have had a successful career at McBain, but unfortunately I could not finish the international relations course because of having to make time for a mandatory internship. Nevertheless, I managed to work with McBain in the US, Mexico and Switzerland, quite an achievement that allowed me to learn and deliver value in business strategy and to understand more about international differences by admiring and respecting them.

As to the social awareness, I first developed interest in social activities while participating with my grandparents in taking care of all the charitable activities and institutions in their small countryside hometown. Not only did I go to events, but I spent many vacations with poor children and the elderly under my grandparents' responsibility. My contact with social work continued when my parents and their friends in São Paulo started taking care of a NGO called *Projeto Sol* (Sun Project) in a slum. I helped them organize the library in a new building and later, as a consultant, I helped them to optimize management activities to better provide for the increasing number of children. In high school and at university, I led initiatives to take poor children to cultural excursions and to help them with their homework. Today, I am part of *Projeto Sol* and of a group that makes donations to a different NGO every month. Because we need to check if the NGOs are in good standing before making the donation, I also learn about different ideas and the difficulties they face in the Brazilian reality.

Wharton-Lauder will give me the opportunity of getting in contact with examples of international business cooperation around social impact activities. The international aspect of the joint-degree will allow me to enlarge my international experience, learn more about the different cultures, realities, businesses and social networks, and enrich my ideas about the theme. My Lauder international exchange in France and Senegal and the classes about language, history and culture will help me understand and value culture and reality differences even more. Seminars with international leaders will improve my understanding of stories of success and failure in entrepreneurship and in coordination among stakeholders with different interests. The Lauder project I intend to do during my first year will be an instrument of studies about success stories of big international social accomplishments such as the World Bank and Save the Children.

Wharton-Lauder will also make me part of a community of potential partners for my future activities, people who already show interest in bigger international feats and who will become part of leading group for change in the world. Lauder community was one of the important factors I considered in my school choice. All the alumni I met work for what they believe and speak of Lauder with shining eyes. Ignacio Pena, a Lauder partner in McBain São Paulo and the partner of my current case, is one of them. Interested in difference, international environment, and community, he is the social impact initiative leader in the office, is always up to date about what is happening outside our work reality, and has admirable values without losing performance in the business side. Renato Matiolli, my colleague and friend at McBain, and his wife Paola are equally enthusiastic about their Lauder experience. I also had the opportunity to spend one afternoon with the Lauder Portuguese track 2012 class during their visit to McBain in São Paulo and I saw a group of people I would like to be part of, with different backgrounds, but the same interest - learning and broadening their minds in an international frame. After talking to them I was even surer Lauder is the course that will make me happy and allow me to prepare for my professional future.

The pursuit of my goal will involve great efforts in increasing my knowledge, improving my transit among the right community and learning to make structural changes in companies, communities, or even countries, and I perceive Wharton-Lauder joint-degree as being the right course to prepare me for this challenge.

Why Lauder #5

Undergraduate Juniors at Wharton have the option to submatriculate into the Wharton graduate program. Those part of the Huntsman Program may naturally choose to submatriculate into the Lauder Program for the same reasons that they initially chose the Huntsman Program. But what was not apparent to me when I was thinking about submatriculating and what is only apparent to me now in hindsight is how valuable work experience is to getting the most out of my MBA. The rationale for why I chose the Huntsman Program is still valid and explains my interest in the Lauder Program, which I will further explain.

By the time of my Junior year I had been in school for 21 years. I was eager to work, to prove myself and see what life was like in the real world. In my job hunt I actually looked for opportunities that would logically relate to my studies. I received an offer from a prestigious Bank's Latin America team, affording me the opportunity to put in practice all that I had learned in the Huntsman Program. Three years ago I switched into the Latin America Debt Capital Markets team and witnessed first hand the effects of a global credit crunch on companies in Mexico and Chile. For the past three years I have helped companies both big and small design financial solutions, helping to ensure solvency in some cases and financing growth leading to job creation in others.

Nevertheless, after four years, I began to realize that my learning on the job will be slowing by the time I start the MBA. I felt that my next step—in order to keep my learning curve steep and channel my skills toward challenges that I will enjoy and offer meaningful impact -- was to directly help people in Latin America, especially by helping businesses grow and creating jobs. That realization and the discussions I had with friends, peers and mentors prompted me to seek a change in the form of returning to receive my MBA. Now I am ready to take my education to new levels. I know that by having had my work experience and particularly in the group that I was in, I will be able to take full advantage of and contribute to classroom discussions, while working with my classmates to maximize the value of our time at Wharton. In fact, I am particularly looking forward to the summer project. Some of my closest friends and best experiences have been while living abroad and I am very much looking forward to another such opportunity. These last few years have been incredibly busy and the majority of my business trips have been lightning-like strikes to Mexico and Chile for meetings or diligence sessions often involving overnight flights, affording me no opportunity to stay and really immerse myself in the culture.

Now after my four years of work experience, I know that going back to graduate school is the right move for me. I view receiving my MBA/MA from Wharton/Lauder as a critical next step in my career, where I will embark on a new life-changing adventure, particularly in the context of Latin America. I hope to capitalize on the diverse experiences of the entire Wharton/Lauder experience such as my Learning Team, cohort, my summer project teams and the guidance of highly energetic professors like Dr. Guillén when my team prepares our research project for the Global Knowledge Lab. I can't stress enough how much I am actually looking forward to all these activities. What impresses me to no end is that Lauder students and alumni especially are not only able to operate the complex business models needed to succeed professionally and personally, but also are able to understand the underlying assumptions and consequences of the models and actions they utilize.

Only through the holistic Lauder perspective (which I have come to appreciate from my Huntsman experience) will I be able to achieve my long-term career vision: to drive development and growth in order to improve the lives of people in Latin America. Additionally, the immersion experience including the intensive language classes, the management consulting project and lectures that go beyond strictly business issues presents the unique possibility to combine two of my passions: I will benefit on a personal level by being able to travel while exploring different ways in which to make an impact on organizations.

The other aspect of the Huntsman Program that I truly value and that I know I will find in the Lauder Program is the tight knit community. To this day, some of my closest friends are the very same people I lived with in Kings Court freshman year. Although it's difficult to stay in touch with everyone when we are all over the world with busy schedules, every so often when someone visits NYC, it's always a cause for us to get together and the email chains for dinner at some new restaurant begin. I've also kept in touch with my Huntsman program adviser. I would always swing by her office during our Penn recruiting visits and even try and hold the actual informational sessions for the Latin America group in the program office. I'd later follow up with her when Huntsman candidates were applying to Penn, looking for ways to backup the Huntsman candidate in the review committee. Helping the Huntsman community is very important to me given everything that the program has given me.

Even though making an impact on organizations is one of my main activities, what I love about Lauder is that it also fits with my passion for history, literature, sociology and many other disciplines. Additionally, the perspectives used in the analysis of the social sciences are often quite different from the models employed in business. Therefore, the subjects that lead to the Master of Arts degree will not only be valuable because of the topics analyzed, but they will also complement the analytical frameworks I will learn in the business school. Moreover, as focused as I may be in Latin America, an increasingly integrated world requires the understanding of local cultures from a global perspective: the mix of global reach and regional specialization which characterizes Lauder is the best mix I can think of. I have learned firsthand from my work at a large Bank that social phenomena clearly shape the development of business which is why I am so enthusiastic of going back to Penn.

For the same reason that I value the tight knit community on a personal level, the network the program will afford me will help me succeed professionally. Just as I have helped Huntsman graduates decide on their future and gain entrance at my Bank, where possible, I know that the Lauder Program, its professors and alumni will also do everything in their power to help me succeed. From a professional and personal perspective, I know that the Lauder Program will help me define and achieve my future career goals. I look forward to discussing my future with you.

Why Lauder #6

The reason I am applying to Lauder is to become fluent in both a language and a culture: Portuguese and Brazilian business. To gain experience in Brazilian business at the depth to which I have experienced doing business in Mexico, Colombia and El Salvador, and to learn Portuguese as well as I know Spanish, would provide me with access to the Latin American business world in its entirety. These experiences will be critical to the success of launching my hybrid-model social enterprise in Latin America (see professional objectives essay). With an economy that is somewhat comparable in size and sophistication to that of Mexico's, Brazil boasts a more cutting-edge culture and a greater international perspective than Mexico, with which I am already familiar after living there for three years. It is absolutely critical for the success of my venture to grow from Mexico to Brazil, given its size and growing power in the global economy. Consequently, the enabler to access the beneficial Brazilian business experiences is the ability to speak Portuguese at an advanced level.

On a personal level, I have wanted to learn Portuguese for many years. Despite my best intentions, I haven't been able to do so given the demands of my career. In speaking with Sol Anitua, an alumna from 2008 who now works in international commodity sales, I was convinced that the Lauder Portuguese program will provide me with the opportunity to become sufficiently fluent in Portuguese to earn respect in business interactions like she has. After three months of interacting in Spanish with the CEO at my Colombian client, I had to present some business recommendations in English for the first time. I was surprised when he commented that my English was remarkable; he had mistaken me for a Mexican. This confirmed that I am not only fluent in the language, but also in the slang, the colloquial phrasings and even the gestures of native Mexicans – the "language" of Mexican business. Once Latinos learn that I am not of Latino descent, they are especially appreciative of my Spanish-speaking abilities. Earning this respect has been not only rewarding, but also invaluable in a business environment. I yearn to develop the same level of fluency in Portuguese in order to be successful in doing business in Brazil.

On a professional level, I believe that the Lauder Portuguese program is the best vehicle by which to gain exposure to the Brazilian business culture while simultaneously developing innovative entrepreneurial skills at Wharton. I will use Lauder's Global Knowledge Lab to combine these two fields of study to explore entrepreneurial ventures in Brazil and in other Latin American countries. If I am to start my business in Mexico and expand it to Brazil (and beyond), the concept will need to be one that is easily transferrable across borders and cultures. I am particularly interested in studying the key success factors of hybrid business models like that of TOMS Shoes, which started in Argentina and has since spread internationally. While TOMS mainly targets affluent American customers on the front end of its "one-to-one" model, it has local operations on the back end that require attentiveness to local nuances for seamless, cross-culture execution. I will use the first summer of my Lauder career in Brazil to identify the existing cross-culture social enterprises in Brazil and begin to plan for my GKL on the concept.

I have also come to a point in my career when I am seeking new sources of inspiration. The past three years of working in investment banking and management consulting have been some of the most enriching experiences of my life. However, the experiences are starting to repeat themselves and I feel like my personal growth is stagnating. I am excited to return to an environment that fosters intellectual discovery of more than just business concepts. Especially because my professional aspirations are dependent on cultural adaptations, I believe that the courses and structure of the Lauder program through which I can explore the cultural, political and global economic history will add the layer of intellectual exploration that I dearly miss and truly believe is the most enriching element of studying business in today's global economy. I feel like I am at the perfect stage in my life to take my ideas, my analytical capabilities and my cross-cultural experiences back to the classroom, where I can combine it all through the Lauder program.

This same intellectual curiosity is what is drove me to request a temporary transfer to San Francisco. I was curious about the differences with other offices, and intrigued by the work done through McBain's Private Equity Group with the cutting-edge clients in Silicon Valley. San Francisco is a center for innovation, and McBain's exposure to venture capital and start-ups in the Bay Area seemed really interesting during a time when I am thinking about ideas for my own business. Coincidentally, my first project here is for a Brazilian client looking to enter the US market. Although my clients speak English, I am thrilled by the opportunity to begin to use Portuguese in a business setting. The alignment of my interests with the McBain's client demands is driving me to enroll in a Portuguese for Spanish speakers course in preparation for the Lauder Portuguese track. I didn't anticipate receiving this type of opportunity until I had earned a joint degree from the Wharton/Lauder Portuguese program, but this project is the perfect stepping stone between my current experience and my future aspirations. It will be a crash course in many aspects of Brazilian business, exposing the areas of opportunity to learn more about Brazilian business culture that I will be able to explore in depth through the Lauder Portuguese program.

BIOGRAPHY

Bredesen (Brett) Lewis was born and raised in New York City. He pursued his undergraduate studies at McGill University. During his summers, Brett worked at the United Nations in New York, volunteered in Mexico, and interned in management consulting in London. Following McGill, Brett completed his MSc in International Political Economy at the London School of Economics.

After graduating from the LSE, Brett pursued his interest in strategy and private equity at Bain & Company. At Bain, Brett worked extensively on private equity due diligences, post-acquisition turnarounds, and corporate strategy.

After two years at Bain, Brett sought to devote more time to the social sector and took a leave of absence to move to San Francisco and work for The Bridgespan Group, a nonprofit consulting firm. While at Bridgespan, Brett worked with a charter school in Los Angeles and a large nonprofit in Washington, DC. After Bridgespan, Brett returned to Bain as a Senior Associate Consultant.

Brett is pursuing a joint Wharton-Lauder MBA and MA. He speaks French, German and Portuguese and interned at Monashees Capital, a Brazilian venture capital fund, in between his first and second year at Wharton.

Brett has always been involved in public service and the arts, primarily with film, theatre, and writing. You can also find Brett diving in warm waters, cooking with friends, and dancing to good music.

All feedback, questions and comments are welcome at bredesenlewis@gmail.com. The occasional insightful comment can be found on Twitter @bredesen.

Bredesen Lewis

Made in the USA
Coppell, TX
08 February 2024

28756885R00083